All About AGILITY

All About

AGILITY

Revised Edition

Jacqueline O'Neil

Howell Book House
New York

Howell Book House

IDG Books Worldwide, Inc.
An International Data Group Company
919 E. Hillsdale Boulevard
Suite 400
Foster City, CA 94404

ISBN: 978-1-62045-761-0

Manufactured in the United States of America

10 9 8 7 6 5 4 3 2

Dedication

To my daughters, Peggy and Sunny Fraser.

You were delightful little girls when I wrote my first book. Now you are charming and independent young women. Thank you for socializing puppies, for being Obedience posts and for riding in the wagon to help the dogs prepare for weight pulls. And thank you especially for blossoming so beautifully, even though you shared your formative years with my dog hobby. Of all the things I have done or won during my life, I am proudest of being your mother.

Acknowledgments

Thank you, agility gurus Dr. Mike Bond and John and Patricia Loomis for sharing your clear, sensible and sensitive wisdom. Both new and seasoned handlers will find your insights indispensable.

Thank you Sharon Anderson, Richard Budney, Harry and Pat Guticz, Charles L. "Bud" Kramer, Stuart Mah, Dr. S. Shane McConnell and Jane Simmons-Moake for answering my questions and sending information and photos. Without your expert help, I could not have completed this book.

Thank you Marilyn Bain and Jean Carter for bringing your enthusiastic dogs to a photo shoot. And special thanks to my husband, Tom O'Neil, for shooting the training photos and cooking super spaghetti sauce when I was glued to the computer.

And a second thank you to Sharon Anderson, AKC's Field Director for Agility, for keeping me up to date on the changes that constantly occur in this new sport and for providing some of the pictures.

Table of Contents

Foreword

I was first introduced to the sport of agility on a cold New Year's Day in 1989. There was an agility demonstration at an obedience match I was attending, and for $2 you could introduce your dog to the equipment. I put my first dog, Shannon, on the course and through the equipment, and at the end I knew we wanted to do more. I was able to attend an agility class later that year. Shortly after that we began competing in agility shows. The rest, as they say, is history.

During that time there were only two organizations that promoted agility: the United States Dog Agility Association (USDAA) and the National Committee for Dog Agility (NCDA, now UKC agility). Both had different performance and judging criteria. There were only a handful of events a year, and you could often go three or four months between events. Agility titles easily took a minimum of a year to complete, and that was only if you almost always qualified. When you went to an event, there was always much to be learned and you almost always "winged it," never knowing quite what to expect.

Today things are a bit different. In the United States alone, we have no less than four organizations that sponsor agility programs. Each program has its own set of rules, regulations and judging criteria. In most parts of the country you can find all four "flavors" of agility on any given weekend, and you could conceivably go to a different type of agility event each week. In addition, the number of events that one can go to has increased at least tenfold. Add to that the fact that countries like Canada and Mexico, our two closet geographical neighbors, put on agility events, and the number of agility events that any person can go to is limited only by finances or time. To earn a title now takes only a fraction of the time that it took 10 years ago.

With the many types of agility and the number of events that you can now attend, things like rules and judging can get to be a bit confusing. Which organizations let you knock down a bar and still qualify? In which organizations is it a fault to miss the up contact of the A-frame? How much time do you have to complete a course? To agility handlers that have been around for awhile, all the agility organizations with their rules and regulations can be merely confusing. To the handlers new to agility, keeping track of all this can be a downright nightmare.

The book you now hold in your hand, *All About Agility*, takes the guesswork and confusion out of keeping track. Jacqueline O'Neil has made it easy by offering concise information on all the organizations, rules, regulations and titles, and offers comparisons of each organization.

In addition to organizations and rules, Jackie offers bountiful information on obstacles and equipment, how to get started, where to go to get started, and what to do once you get started. Chapter 5, "Agility Events" is especially helpful to people new to agility. Jackie tells you what you need to know to start participating in agility and what to expect when you go to an event. Knowing what to do, where to go, what to expect and what to bring to agility events is something I wish I'd had when I began showing. It would have taken away much of the guesswork and headaches that I had to go through in my early years. Now, new agility handlers can go to an agility event with the confidence of a seasoned competitor.

Finally, Chapter 6, "Training Tips from the Pros" is nice in that you can "talk" to a few more experienced competitors and get answers to some frequently asked questions.

All in all, *All About Agility*, is a one-stop agility book, covering much of what you need to know before you get hooked! Happy reading and clean runs to all.

Stuart Mah
Jacksonville, Florida 1999

Active in agility since 1989, Stuart Mah has excelled as a competitor, an instructor and a judge. He has represented the United States five times in international competition. He is a noted author and a leading expert in course design. In 1996, Stuart was voted the USDAA Agility Person of the Year.

The Most Fun You Can Have with Your Dog

Agility is the epitome of exciting teamwork. Thrilling to participants and spectators, it blends desire, control, training and athletic ability into a rip-roaring good time. The object of agility is for a handler to direct his or her dog over a timed obstacle course without the dog making a mistake such as bumping a jump or missing a weave pole. Dogs leap colorful hurdles, hustle through tunnels, take a turn on the see-saw and hasten up and down ramps on courses that resemble playgrounds and are never the same twice.

All healthy dogs can enjoy agility. It doesn't matter if they are purebred or mixed-bred, large or small, young or middle-aged. Through agility training, dogs release their energy constructively and learn how to be under control and in high spirits at the same time. Agility dogs and their owners are better than best friends. They are partners.

Every dog owner can enjoy agility, too. It doesn't matter if you are young or old, quick or slow, graceful or clumsy. If you have a sense of humor, or wish you could find the one you lost, a world of fun awaits you. Would you like to build a better bond with your dog? Make new friends? Travel to new places? Accept new challenges? You can do it all through the sport of agility. Best of all, you can set your own goals and accomplish them on your own schedule.

Welcome to agility, a game so captivating that a short demonstration spawned an international sport.

How much fun is agility?

Ask anyone who's tried it and you'll get the same answer: Agility is the most fun you can have with your dog.

Judy Iby sends Cory through the tire. When agility first became popular, Judy wanted to try it but didn't think she could because she has a herniated disk and has had knee surgery three times. But the sport looked like so much fun that she couldn't resist. Since then she's put nine agility titles on her dogs (of course, the fact that they were already dog show champions with obedience and tracking titles helped). "Yes, you can teach old dogs new tricks," Judy says. "Agility training gives new life to senior citizens." Judy says that includes both her retired dogs and herself, and claims agility training helped her health.

CHAPTER 1

WHAT IS *Agility?*

Agility is a spectator sport where dogs are timed as they navigate an obstacle course at the direction of their handlers. The course resembles a huge playground and usually includes a see-saw, hurdles, tunnels, ramps of various configurations and weave poles. In the Introduction, I welcomed you to a game so captivating that a short demonstration spawned an international sport. Here's how it happened.

THE ORIGIN OF AGILITY

Agility is a young sport. It began in 1978 when John Varley, a member of the committee that puts on the Crufts Dog Show in England, needed an exhibition to entertain the spectators during the break between two main events. A horseman as well as a dog fancier, he envisioned dogs negotiating obstacles and jumping hurdles similar to those used in equestrian events. So Varley and his friend, Peter Meanwell, designed the first agility course and invited a few dog owners to train their dogs for the upcoming demonstration.

Several months later, two teams, each composed of four dogs and handlers, entered the arena at the Crufts show and awed the audience with their dexterity, speed and control. One by one, the dogs soared over hurdles, scampered through tunnels and scaled planks at their handler's direction. The spectators shouted encouragement and a sport was born. There was only one thing the thousands of dog lovers in that audience wanted to do more than watch agility: They wanted to try it with their own dogs. And they soon did.

It wasn't long before The Kennel Club in England recognized agility, making it a standard competitive event with its own set of regulations. The new sport drew thousands of participants and a following of enthusiastic spectators. Today, major British competitions are often televised and the sport has spread all over the world.

AGILITY COMES TO AMERICA

Every year Americans attend British dog shows, especially prestigious ones like Crufts, and when these travelers arrived home they told their friends about the exciting new sport. But Kenneth Tatsch of Richardson, Texas, went a step further. With help from British experts, he erected agility courses according to English regulations and introduced the sport in the United States. In 1985, Tatsch founded the United States Dog Agility Association (USDAA).

Charles "Bud" Kramer of Manhattan, Kansas, created a different type of agility course and founded the National Club for Dog Agility (NCDA) in 1987. The North American Dog Agility Council (NADAC) was also established during the late '80s, using the British style, but with variations.

The American Kennel Club (AKC) recognized agility as a performance event under its own set of regulations in 1994, sparking yet another surge in the sport's popularity. More than 600 AKC trials were held across the country in 1998, with 143,828 dog entered and 7,790 of them earning titles. In 1995 the United Kennel Club (UKC) sanctioned agility using the NCDA style, and their trials were also an immediate success.

TWENTY YEARS OF CHANGE

Agility originally favored fleet dogs of the medium to large breeds and their equally speedy handlers, so how did it become a sport for dogs and handlers of all shapes and sizes? One major change dealt with the height of the hurdles. All agility jumps were originally 30 inches high, but today every agility organization in the United States accommodates different size dogs by offering several jump height divisions. The amount of speed needed to succeed has also changed, reflecting the philosophies of different agility organizations.

Each of the several organizations offering agility today has a different emphasis and its own regulations. Keeping them all straight may seem complicated at first, but the variety adds up to good news for you. No matter what kind of dog your Beau is (purebred or mixed, eager or easygoing), and no matter what type of handler you are (competitive or laid-back), at least one type of agility will fit you just fine. Beau can earn agility titles whether he is a Basset Hound or a Border Collie.

But don't get the impression that agility has been toned down, because it hasn't. These days, exceptionally quick and graceful dogs won't have time to be bored. Challenges abound for good trainers with dogs of the "born agile" breeds, and how high you strive is your decision. Besides titles, there are class placements, championships, tournaments and a variety of solo, pair and team competitions at all levels of difficulty. In fact, agility has become such an international sport that teams from 23 countries, including France, Japan, Germany, Italy, Russia, Israel, Africa and the United States, converged on Maribor, Slovenia, for the World Agility Championship in 1998. That's quite a field for such a young sport, and even more countries are preparing teams to compete in the future.

In the next chapter you'll find out what the agility organizations have in common, as well as their major differences. Some of you won't even have to make a decision. Many well-trained agility dogs successfully compete at the event closest to them, no matter which organization sanctions it. Other dog-handler pairs travel far afield to participate in their favorite sport.

Being short-legged doesn't slow Bandit down as he bounds up the A-frame. He's owned by Jean Carter of Kalispell, Montana.

CHAPTER 2

AGILITY *Organizations*

The big three organizations offering agility in the United States are the United States Dog Agility Association, Inc. (USDAA), the United Kennel Club (UKC), which adopted the style originated by the National Club for Dog Agility (NCDA), and the American Kennel Club (AKC). Several other excellent but smaller organizations also offer agility competitions, and are listed in the Appendix.

HOW ARE THEY THE SAME?

Each agility organization offers titles to successful dogs at various levels of difficulty, is concerned with safety, and provides a good time for the dogs, handlers and spectators. No matter which organization's event you enter, you can count on running the obstacle course solo (one handler and dog team at a time), while your dog is both judged and timed.

Beau will be off-lead and you will not be permitted to touch him, but you may give both verbal and signal commands, handle from either side and change sides at will. No treats, toys or other training aids will be allowed on the course.

Obstacles will include a variety of hurdles, tunnels, a pause table or box and contact obstacles (in Chapter 3 we'll look at each type of obstacle in depth).

HOW ARE THEY DIFFERENT?

Understanding the differences between the organizations will help you decide which agility style will be best for you and Beau.

The differences start with philosophy. The USDAA considers agility a spectator sport, and prides itself on promoting the international standards of agility originally developed in Great Britain. These standards, which have become the basis for the world standard, feature spacious courses and emphasize speed as well as accuracy and control. USDAA agility uses more obstacles in its Novice classes and slightly higher obstacles in general, but after Beau learns this somewhat more demanding style of agility, he can easily make the transition to AKC courses. He can also succeed at UKC events once he has been introduced to smaller, tighter courses and a few obstacles unique to UKC agility. Beau is eligible for USDAA registration

A Border Terrier owned and handled by 10-year-old Elizabeth Ridley, clears a jump with room to spare. Jump heights make more of a difference to some dogs than to others.

WHY THE RULES MAY CHANGE

Because it is a new sport, agility is still evolving. Each organization reviews its regulations periodically and occasionally makes minor alterations. Jump heights, for example, have already undergone several revisions and will probably be debated for years. The heights given here are correct as I'm writing, but consult the official rule book of the organization under which you plan to compete to make sure they are still correct when you are reading.

A dog's height is measured from the ground to its withers. Odie measured 21 inches.

Rule books undergo revisions too, so always keep current. Other requirements may also change.

One thing that won't change is how a dog's height is measured. It is measured from the floor to the withers—the highest point of the shoulder blades, found just behind the base of the neck—and jump heights for each dog are determined by this measurement.

whether he is a purebred or a mixed-bred. He must be at least 18 months old to compete.

The UKC places an emphasis on precision and control rather than speed and hurdle height. The UKC's objective is to offer a style of agility where all handlers, regardless of physical abilities, and all dogs, no matter what their breed characteristics, have an equal opportunity to achieve success. It fulfills this goal by using lower hurdles and permitting slower course times than the other two organizations, while demanding more exacting performances.

If Beau is trained in UKC agility he will be proficient in a wide variety of obstacles. He may also succeed in AKC and USDAA events, provided he is introduced gradually to higher hurdles and is physically capable of running the longer USDAA courses at a brisk pace. Beau may be registered with the UKC to participate in agility whether he is a purebred or a mixed-bred, and must be at least six months old to compete.

AKC agility was formulated to give dogs of every AKC-registrable breed an opportunity to demonstrate their willingness to work in partnership with their handlers under a variety of conditions. Its courses and regulations put it

REGULATION HURDLE HEIGHT DIVISIONS

	Height of Dog at Withers	Jump Height
USDAA	12 inches or less	12 inches
	16 inches or less	16 inches
	21 inches or less	22 inches
	over 21 inches	26 inches
UKC	14 inches and under	8 inches
	over 14 inches but under 20 inches	14 inches
	over 20 inches	20 inches
AKC	10 inches and under	8 inches
	14 inches and under	12 inches
	18 inches and under	16 inches
	22 inches and under	20 inches
	over 22 inches	24 inches

between the speedier, more competitive USDAA style and the slower, more controlled UKC program. While AKC obstacles are similar to USDAA obstacles, AKC hurdles are slightly lower and assigned course times are five seconds slower. After Beau masters AKC agility he should be able to succeed in UKC events, once he is introduced to the obstacles unique to UKC courses.

He may also do fine at USDAA events, provided he gets used to jumping a little higher and moving a little faster. To be eligible for AKC agility trials, Beau must be an AKC-registered purebred dog at least 12 months old. Breeds in the Miscellaneous Class may also compete in AKC agility.

CLASSES FOR BEGINNERS

Each agility organization has classes for dogs and handlers who are just getting started. These beginners' classes have different names and slightly different requirements, but all are designed to get you started and get you hooked on agility.

BEGIN AT THE BEGINNING

	USDAA	UKC	AKC
What trial class should a beginner enter?	Starters	Agility I	Novice
What should Beau wear when competing?	Nothing; dogs may not wear a collar when competing.	A plain buckle collar is required while competing.	Beau may run with or without a collar. If he wears one, it must be a plain buckle collar.
How many obstacles are there on beginner courses?	14 to 16	13	12 or 13

Obstacles on Beginner Courses

On USDAA Starters and Novice classes, obstacles include the collapsed tunnel, open or pipe tunnel, pause table, see-saw (teeter-totter), weave poles, tire jump and a variety of jumps, including a double or triple bar jump or a broad jump.

(By the way, the USDAA Starters and Novice courses are identical. Sign up for Starters if you have never handled a dog to an agility title. It's for untitled dogs and new handlers. Novice is also for untitled dogs, but the handler may be a veteran who has put agility titles on several dogs.)

In the UKC Agility I class, obstacles include the dog walk, A-frame, see-saw (teeter-totter), closed tunnel, open or pipe tunnel, hoop tunnel, pause table and six hurdles.

In the AKC Novice class, obstacles include the dog walk, A-frame, see-saw (teeter-totter), closed tunnel, open tunnel, pause table, tire or window jump and a series of hurdles including the panel jump (solid wall jump), the broad jump and the double bar jump (double oxer).

Course Times

You and Beau will be timed at agility trials and must complete the premeasured course within a specified time to avoid a time penalty. Here's how each orga-nization arrives at the time limit for its beginners class.

In the USDAA Starters and Novice classes, the standard course time (SCT) may be no less than two yards per second. Also, the maximum stan-dard course time is 75 seconds.

Assigned course times (ACT) for UKC Agility I range from 60 to 98 seconds, depending upon the size and structure of the dog, and the length and difficulty of the course. Maximum course time may be called at the judges' discretion if a dog takes more than double the assigned course time.

The course time for the AKC Novice class is two yards per second, plus an additional five seconds for the pause table. Maximum course time is one and a half times the designated course time.

Penalties

In all cases, Beau begins his run of the course with a perfect score. Then, penalties are given for time and performance faults. A few examples of course faults are given here, but what is considered a faulty performance varies from one agility organization to another. For a complete list of each organization's course faults and how much Beau will be penalized for each one, check each national organization's rule book.

In USDAA trials, various course faults, such as knocking the bar off a jump or missing a contact zone (an area the dog is required to touch with at least one paw; more on that in Chapter 3), are five-point penalties every time they occur. Missing an obstacle completely is a 20-point penalty. In addi-tion, time is tallied to the hundredth of a second. For example, if Beau takes

92.3 seconds to perform a course with an SCT of 90 seconds, his time fault is 2.3 seconds. If he also entered the open tunnel from the wrong end, he would have a five-point course penalty as well. The two penalties added together equal a total penalty of 7.3.

UKC course faults may be assessed as major or minor, depending on how serious they are. For example, if you send Beau to an obstacle and he stops dead in front of it, then decides to give it a go and succeeds in negotiating it, the judge may deduct one or two points for a minor course fault. But if Beau backs away from the obstacle and you have to circle and send him all over again, the penalty may be increased by a point or two. Time faults are judged by hundredths of a second. So, if the assigned course time was 74 seconds and Beau ran it in 75.6 seconds, he would have a time penalty of 1.6, which would be added to his course penalties.

In AKC trials, time is also measured to the nearest one-hundredth of a second, but when assessing time penalties, fractions are rounded down to the nearest whole second. Dogs are penalized one point for every second they go over course time (counting only whole numbers). So, if the assigned course time is 80 seconds and Beau runs it in 80.4, he would not receive a time penalty. Points are also deducted for course faults. For example, if Beau leaves the pause table (see Chapter 3) too soon and has to hop back on it and start over, he will receive a two-point course penalty.

Scoring Systems

No matter which organization sanctions the trial, if Beau runs the course up to that organization's high standard of performance, he will receive a qualifying score. In agility jargon, a qualifying score gives Beau a "leg" toward a title. What's a title? It's letters that become part of Beau's name, signifying that he has been educated in agility to a certain level and proved it by passing tests—like a person becoming a D.V.M. or a Ph.D. As you will see, each organization has its own agility titles and distinct requirements for earning them. Here's how they will score Beau's performance.

Under USDAA rules, Beau starts his run with a perfect score of zero. If he has course faults (performs an obstacle out of sequence, for example), or time faults (goes over the standard course time), he will not earn a leg toward an agility title. If he has a clear run (agility jargon for a faultless performance) and finishes within the standard course time, he will be awarded a leg toward his agility title.

At UKC trials, Beau will begin with a perfect score of 200 points. If he finishes the course with 170 points or more and no nonqualifying faults, he will earn a leg toward his agility title. Points are lost through major and minor course faults, and by taking longer than the assigned course time.

Beau will begin his run with 100 points at AKC trials, and may lose some of them along the way to course and/or time faults. If he still has 85 or more points when he finishes, and has no nonqualifying deductions, he will qualify for a leg.

That Fabulous First Title

The first USDAA title is Agility Dog (AD), as in Beau, AD. To earn it, Beau has to earn three legs by running three clear rounds under at least two different judges in the Starters and/or the Novice class.

The first UKC title is Agility I (U-AGI), as in Beau, U-AGI. Three qualifying scores (170 or better with no nonqualifying faults) are required in the Agility I class, and they may be awarded by one, two or three judges.

The first AKC title is Novice Agility (NA), as in Beau, NA. To earn it, Beau needs three qualifying scores (85 or better with no nonqualifying faults) in the Novice class, awarded by at least two different judges.

MORE TITLES AND CLASSES

Each agility organization offers advanced titles in their standard classes. (In agility jargon, standard classes are those where the dog runs a regular agility course.) The obstacle course and time limits become progressively more difficult as dogs move up the ranks.

Besides standard classes, some organizations hold nonstandard classes, called novelty classes, where the course is altered to emphasize strategy, jumping ability or distance control. Occasionally team competitions are offered. Whenever these additional classes are available, it always adds to the fun.

USDAA

In addition to the Agility Dog (AD) title, USDAA offers:

Advanced Agility Dog (AAD)   Awarded to dogs after they earn three qualifying scores in the Advanced Agility class. Earning the AAD proves Beau successfully ran moderately difficult courses and you've succeeded in performing some complex handling maneuvers as a team.

Master Agility Dog (MAD)   Respectfully known as Mad Dog, the MAD is awarded to dogs after they have clear rounds on the challenging

Master course three times and earn a qualifying score in four nonstandard classes: Gamblers, Jumpers, Snookers and Pairs Relay. Earning the coveted MAD proves Beau is not only exceptionally accomplished in agility, but is versatile as well.

Gamblers   This novelty class tests your strategy, as well as Beau's speed and distance control. Instead of taking the obstacles in order, as you would during a standard agility class, you will send Beau to the obstacles of your choice in whatever order you choose. The challenge is to see how many obstacles Beau can navigate in a specified amount of time, as points are awarded for each obstacle. You may take each obstacle up to twice in either direction, and more points are earned for contact obstacles than for hurdles (because they take longer and are harder to execute perfectly).

When the time whistle blows, you may leave the course with the points Beau has already earned or try the final gamble (sometimes called the "joker"). It will be a series of three or more obstacles that Beau has to negotiate quickly and all by himself, as you must remain in place after giving the command or signal. If Beau succeeds at the gamble he will gain bonus points, but if he makes a mistake he will lose points. The winner is the dog with the most points, and ties are decided by the fastest time.

Advanced "gamblers" may try the Masters Gamblers class. When they earn five qualifying scores, they will be awarded the title Gamblers Master.

Jumpers   In this nonstandard class, the course consists entirely of different types of hurdles, which must be jumped within the time limit. Dogs are penalized for performance errors and time faults, and the dog with the least faults wins. To achieve the Jumpers Master title, Beau needs five qualifying scores in the challenging Masters Jumpers class.

Snookers   Quick and competitive, the agility game called Snookers has an opening and a closing sequence and a time limit. (In agility jargon, a sequence is a series of obstacles performed one after the other.) Each obstacle is assigned a color and each color is worth a designated number of points. For example, there may be a red obstacle worth three points, a blue one worth eight points, and so on.

During the opening sequence you may select some of the obstacles, but during the closing sequence Beau must perform the six different colored obstacles in a specified order. Each obstacle in the final sequence is worth more points than the previous obstacle, and the challenge is to accomplish as many as possible, without a fault, before time is up. If Beau makes a mistake or time is called, his run is over and he will leave the ring with the points earned before the error. The dog with the most points wins.

To earn the title Snookers Master, Beau has to qualify five times in the Masters Snooker class, and place in the top 15 percent of the class three of those times.

Pairs or Team Relays   The lowest score wins in relay events, and scores are figured by adding the fault penalties to the time each dog took to run the course. Both dog's scores are added together in pairs relay, and the whole team's scores are added together in team events.

Most relays are done in pairs with the handlers carrying a baton that they must pass off to the next competitor. At some events both handlers run the entire course, while at other events the course is divided. On divided courses, the first handler completes a designated portion of the course, then races back to the start line and passes the baton to the second handler, who completes the second part of the course.

Beau can earn the Relay Master title by qualifying five times in the Masters Relay class with five different partners.

Agility Dog Champion   Only fast, versatile dogs with superb coordination and excellent distance control become Agility Dog Champions. To qualify, Beau has to earn the Master Agility Dog title as well as the titles Jumpers Master, Gamblers Master, Snookers Master and Relay Master.

Yes, it is possible. Twenty-eight dogs became USDAA Agility Dog Champions in 1996. Six of them were mixed-breds, five were Border Collies, five Shetland Sheepdogs, three Jack Russell Terriers, three Miniature Schnauzers and one Chesapeake Bay Retriever, one Golden Retriever, one Labrador Retriever, one Toy Poodle, one Portuguese Water Dog and one Tibetan Terrier. How's that for variety in achieving agility's most demanding title?

Veteran Agility Dog   Is Beau seven years of age or older? Then he's eligible to earn his Veteran Agility Dog title on Novice to Advanced level courses with lower jumps, a lower A-frame and no spread hurdles. Three qualifying scores will do it.

Performance Program   Would you rather have Beau compete on a course with lower jumps and a lower A-frame? The USDAA'S Performance Program features jump heights of 8 inches, 12 inches 16 inches and 22 inches, with the A-frame set at 66 inches. That may be a big help if Beau is a heavier bodied breed. Nonstandard classes are available at three levels.

Junior Handler Classes   USDAA has a junior handlers program for school-age children and offers certificates for JH-Beginner, JH-Elementary, JH-Intermediate and JH-Senior. Three qualifying scores are needed at every level except Beginner, where only one qualifying score is required.

LOTS OF TITLES

	AKC
NA	Novice Agility
OA	Open Agility
AX	Agility Excellent
MX	Master Agility Excellent
NAJ	Novice Jumpers With Weaves
OAJ	Open Jumpers With Weaves
AXJ	Excellent Jumpers With Weaves
MXJ	Master Excellent Jumpers With Weaves
MACH	Master Agility Champion
	UKC
U-AGI	Agility I
U-AGII	Agility II
U-ATCH	Agility Trial Champion
U-ACHX	Agility Champion Excellent
	USDAA
AD	Agility Dog
AAD	Advanced Agility Dog
MAD	Masters Agility Dog
JM	Jumpers Master
GM	Gamblers Master
SM	Snookers Master
RM	Relay Master
VAD	Veteran Agility Dog
ADCH	Agility Dog Champion

UKC

In addition to the U-AGI title, the UKC offers:

Agility II   Sixteen obstacles make up the Agility II course: eight are hurdles, one is a pause box and seven are something other than hurdles and will be different from the obstacles used for Agility I. The course design is also more challenging than the entry-level class. When Beau earns qualifying scores three times in Agility II, he will be awarded the title U-AGII.

Agility Trial Champion (U-ATCH)   To earn this title, Beau has to do better than qualify—he has to perform with finesse. Dogs earn champion points for exceptionally high scores in Agility I and Agility II classes, and when they have 100 points they are awarded their championship. It doesn't take long if Beau performs with control and seldom makes mistakes. A perfect score of 200 is worth 10 points toward a championship. Six points are awarded for scores of 199, four points for 198, two for 197 and one point for a score of 196.

Agility III   Where does a UKC Agility Trial Champion go? Into Agility III classes. In fact, only dogs that have earned their U-ACH are eligible to compete in Agility III. Course designs are more complex, but there won't be any obstacles you haven't seen in Agility I or II. Three qualifying scores and Beau will have his Agility Champion Excellent (U-ACHX) title.

AKC

In addition to the NA title, the AKC offers:

Open Agility (OA)   With 15 to 17 obstacles, including weave poles, a more intricate course design and a faster course time, Beau will find the Open course considerably more difficult than the Novice course. When he qualifies three times under at least two different judges, he will be awarded the OA title and certificate.

Agility Excellent (AX)   The AKC's toughest courses feature 18 to 20 obstacles, a complex design and a faster course time than demanded in the Open class. Three qualifying scores under at least two different judges will earn Beau his AX.

Master Agility Excellent (MX)   Consistency is the key to earning the AKC's highest agility title. Beau becomes an MX by qualifying in the Agility Excellent class 10 more times after earning his AX.

Novice Jumpers With Weaves (NAJ)   This exciting class showcases speed while still demanding control. The course is made up of 13 to 15 obstacles, most of which are jumps. Six weave poles are mandatory and tunnels are permitted. What's unique about the course is that contact obstacles and pause tables are not included, so the dogs and handlers don't have to slow down to negotiate them. Three qualifying scores under two different judges and Beau will have his NAJ.

Open Jumpers With Weaves (OAJ)   With 16 to 18 obstacles, including six to 12 weave poles and a triple bar jump (but nothing to slow you down), the Open Jumpers With Weaves class offers additional challenges to help you and Beau hone your teamwork. Beau will have earned his OAJ when he qualifies three times under two different judges.

Excellent Jumpers With Weaves (AXJ)   The AKC's most advanced Jumpers With Weaves class has 18 to 20 obstacles, including at least 10 to 12 weave poles. Expect several advanced challenges along the way, including some tricky angles approaching the obstacles. Three qualifying scores under two different judges and Beau will have his AXJ.

Master Excellent Jumpers With Weaves (MXJ)   Earning the AKC's top Jumpers With Weaves title requires a combination of consistency and ability. After acquiring the AXJ, Beau can complete his MXJ by accumulating 10 additional qualifying scores in the Excellent Jumpers With Weaves Class.

Master Agility Champion (MACH)   The AKC's most prestigious agility title was created to recognize superior agility dogs. Since stellar performance requires speed and consistency, dogs are awarded a point for each full second they finish under th estandard course time, and can earn those points in the Master Agility Excellent class and the Master Excellent Jumpers With Weaves class. A first-place class win doubles the score. When Beau accumulates 750 points and double qualifies 20 times (has perfect scores of 100, also known as clear rounds, in both MX and MXJ on the same day), he will be awarded the distinguished MACH. What? You and Beau aren't ready to retire yet. Then do it all over again and Beau will become a MACH2.

Junior Handling   The AKC's Junior Handling program recognizes young people between the ages of 10 and 18 who earn titles by handling their dog (or the family dog) in the class in which it would normally compete at an AKC event. First you have to fill out a form. Get yours by calling AKC's Judges Education Department at (919) 854-0195 or e-mail mbo@akc.org.

CONTACTING THE NATIONAL ORGANIZATIONS

Would you like to find a club near you that offers agility lessons and events? Are you ready to read the regulations? Do you want to receive agility publications? Here's how.

United States Dog Agility Association, Inc.
P.O. Box 850955
Richardson, TX 75085-0955
Telephone: (972) 231-9700
Fax: (214) 503-0161
E-mail: info@usdaa.com

Contact USDAA for help in locating an agility group in your area. When you join USDAA, you will receive their rules and regulations, a booklet on training tips, a membership decal and the bimonthly publication *USDAA Dog Agility Report*. This newsletter contains articles on training and will keep you current on upcoming agility events and modifications to the regulations.

United Kennel Club
100 East Kilgore Rd.
Kalamazoo, MI 49001-5598
Telephone: (616) 343-9020, ask for the all-breed department
Fax: (616) 343-7037

The UKC publishes a bimonthly magazine called *Bloodlines*, which lists upcoming agility events across the country and frequently contains agility articles and updates on the regulations. If you would like a sample issue, send $4.50 to the address above. Rule books are also $4.50.

American Kennel Club
5580 Centerview Dr., Suite 200
Raleigh, NC 27606-3390
Telephone: (919) 233-9767
Fax: (919) 233-3627
E-mail: INFO@akc.org

Ask for *Regulations for Agility Trials* and help in locating an agility club near you. Both are free. You may want to subscribe to the AKC's monthly magazine, *AKC Gazette*, which often has articles about agility and updates on the regulations, or check out the AKC's Web site at http:\\www.akc.org. (Dogs must be AKC-registered purebreds or have AKC Limited Registration to participate in AKC agility events. If your dog is not registered, but is an AKC-registrable breed, inquire about obtaining an Indefinite Listing Privilege for the purpose of competing in agility.)

North American Dog Agility Council (NADAC)
HCR 2, Box 277
St. Maries, Idaho 83861
Telephone: (208) 689-3803
Web site: http://www.teleport.com/~jhaglund/nadachom.htm

While not as well known as the big three, NADAC is definitely worth looking into, as there are nearly 50 NADAC clubs in North America. The organization was created by agility enthusiasts so people would have more opportunities to run their dogs and enjoy the sport. Enjoyment is one of NADAC's priorities. Safety is another. The organization offers moderate jump heights and safe course designs (no sharp turns, for example). Dogs must be 18 months of age to compete and the only obstacles permitted at NADAC events are the dog walk or crossover, A-frame, teeter-totter (see-saw), closed tunnel, open tunnel, weave poles, pause table, tire jump, double-bar spread hurdles and winged and nonwinged single hurdles. NADAC offers certificates in three levels of regular competition (Novice, Open and Elite), including classes for Veterans (older dogs) and Junior Handling (youngsters handling the dogs). Their nonregular classes include Gamblers and Jumpers, and their highest certificate is the NADAC Agility Trial Champion (NATCH).

WHAT ABOUT WINNING?

At AKC, UKC and USDAA trials, dogs are awarded first through fourth place in each division, in addition to earning legs for titles. That means you can enjoy agility as a noncompetitive sport if your goal is putting a title after Beau's name—or, you can let your competitive spirit soar by setting your sights on winning the class. How do the organizations decide on the winner?

Under USDAA rules, awards are given for first through fourth place and are determined by the fastest time for a clear round.

*The new AKC Jumpers With Weaves classes emphasize the weave poles and jumps.
This suits Elizabeth and her dog just fine!*

At both AKC and UKC trials, first-through fourth-place awards are presented to the qualifying dogs with the highest scores. In case of a tie, the dog with the faster time wins.

THROUGH AN INSTRUCTOR'S EYES

We've looked at all the obstacles and titles and scoring systems. But what about the intangibles? What's it *really* like to compete at the different levels under different rules?

Agility judge Mike Bond of Naperville, Illinois, runs a private agility training school, Creekwood Meadows Agility, and is co-founder of the AKC Agility Ability Club of Illinois and the UKC Agility Ability Club. He believes each type of agility has its merits and trains for all styles, depending on the skill and aptitude of the handler and dog. Here's how he compares the popular forms of agility:

USDAA generally has a nice flow, allowing dogs to open up and go. Courses spread out nicely. This is a fast style, so dogs and handlers need to be in shape and conditioned. USDAA offers games in addition to the standard class and titles. Jumpers and Gamblers give dog-handler teams an opportunity to test various skills. Some negatives from my perspective are: considerably higher jumps, which can make the competitive career of some large dogs rather short-lived; higher, narrower contact equipment (particularly the dog walk), making this a safety concern; and sometimes an overemphasis on higher, faster and further, that can compromise the canine partner.

NADAC generally has nice flow and exciting courses, too. The style is similar to USDAA. Important differences, however, are lower jump heights (24 inches is maximum for large dogs versus 30 inches maximum in USDAA). NADAC is also a rapid form of agility with a nice balance between jumps, tunnels and contact obstacles. Contact obstacles are wider than USDAA's, making for safer equipment. This style also has agility games, in addition to the standard classes for titles.

AKC's style is similar to NADAC's with a nice balance of jumps, tunnels and contact obstacles. Jump heights are reasonable (identical to NADAC's) and course times are fast but reasonable. This style also offers games at some events, in addition to the standard title classes.

All of the above styles require good-sized venues. Ten thousand square feet is preferable. The emphasis is on course flow, allowing for more speed. The amount of space necessary to set up such a course may be a problem in areas that are limited by space or climate as to when and where they can hold trials.

The fourth style of agility popular in the United States is UKC, formerly known as NCDA. UKC puts more emphasis on control than speed, and courses have more control-type obstacles than hurdles. Course times tend to be slower, jumps are lower and the courses fit into a smaller venue. This allows trials to be held in smaller indoor arenas in areas where climate and space present a problem. Some negatives of this style are inconsistencies with course design and judging. Course flow is sometimes sacrificed in favor of over-control. The previous three styles have established judges' education programs, while the UKC is still working on theirs, making for inconsistencies in judging from place to place.

There are merits to each style. I use UKC work to emphasize control and obstacle discrimination and the other three to accentuate distance and speed. I also use the UKC style to start younger dogs, and return to it toward the end of their competitive careers because lower hurdles and slower course times are kinder to both developing and aging bodies. It's also helpful during the doldrums of winter because it can be practiced in the smaller indoor venues.

For the bulk of my own dogs' competitive careers, and during acceptable weather, I like to train the other three styles and let them open up and go. A nice mix in training is important. It gets me a canine partner that can turn it on and also rein it in and be controlled.

CHAPTER 3

MEET THE *Obstacles*

Many agility obstacles are adapted from equestrian events, and their names reflect their horsey heritage. Other designs were borrowed from police and military K-9 obstacle courses and search-and-rescue training equipment.

All the obstacles commonly used at agility trials are included in this chapter, but you'll never find them all on one course. Some are seen only at advanced levels of competition, and several are used by some agility organizations but not by others. Each organization's rule book will tell you which obstacles it uses on which types of courses.

Agility obstacles fit into a few broad categories, and the same obstacle often has more than one name. I'll include the terms and names in common usage so you'll be able to speak the language of any agility organization you choose.

When introducing Beau to the obstacles, keep him stimulated by doing at least three different ones every time you train. A contact obstacle, a jump and a tunnel add up to an interesting session. If Beau is a beginner, start with the A-frame, the panel jump and the open tunnel and add other obstacles as he demonstrates his readiness. For example, if he is slow learning the A-frame but flies over the first hurdle and barrels through the open tunnel, add a second hurdle and introduce the closed tunnel while continuing to teach the A-frame. Plan your practices so both of you have fun. If you are bored, Beau is probably bored too, and it's time to try an easy new obstacle and come back to the harder one later.

A good instructor is an enormous asset when training your dog for agility, but a bit of background information is always a plus. Here's enough information about each obstacle to get you off to a good start.

WALKING THE PLANKS

The A-frame, cross-over, dog walk, see-saw and sway bridge are all obstacles made of planks or ramps. They are collectively known as contact obstacles or go-ups. All of these obstacles have two things in common:

- Dogs negotiate them by first climbing, and then descending, an inclined plank.

- Every inclined plank has a contact zone—an area a few feet from the ground that dogs are required to touch with at least one paw. These zones keep dogs safe and prove they are under control. Dogs trained to touch contact zones don't leap on or off obstacles from dangerous heights or unsafe angles. Contact zones are always brightly painted and are a different color (usually yellow) than the rest of the obstacle.

The height, width and steepness of the contact obstacles depend upon each agility organization's regulations.

A-Frame
Shaped like a capital A, the A-frame has wide planks on both sides and is crossed with sturdy chain or wooden braces to keep it stable. It has contact zones on the lower few feet of each side.

Beau will perform the A-frame correctly if he approaches it from the designated side and scampers up one side and down the other without missing a contact zone. (Note: In AKC agility he has to touch the contact zone on the downward side only.)

Stepping Off on the Right Paw
It's okay to introduce Beau to the A-frame when he is still a pup, but no matter how young or old he is, the obstacle should be flat on the ground or inclined only slightly until he is comfortable with it. The first step is getting him familiar with the obstacle, and the best method depends upon his temperament. No one knows Beau better than you, so choose the technique you

think will fit. If it doesn't work, no problem. Just stop doing it that way and try a different method.

One way to introduce Beau to the A-frame is to guide him across with one hand on his lead while the other hand holds a treat just in front of his nose. Give him the goodie as soon as he completes the obstacle and is back on solid ground. Another method is to have a helper hold Beau while you go to the opposite end of the A-frame and look at him over the top (if it is inclined slightly), or simply stand at the other end (if it is flat on the ground). Then call him in a happy, excited voice. Your helper should release Beau as soon as he is totally focused on you. When he crosses the A-frame and is back on the ground, greet him with a hug and a treat.

If Beau is nervous on the A-frame (he either balks, hesitates or runs across it wildly in an effort to get it over with quickly), try walking across it with him. Just be sure to stay to one side because you want him to get into the habit of staying in the middle. If that isn't enough to relax Beau, sit beside him on the A-frame for several minutes of petting.

Still having a problem? Never underestimate the benefits of letting Beau observe a dog that obviously loves the game. Many a nervous dog changed his attitude after watching another dog have fun on an obstacle. Ask the handler of an eager dog to take his or her dog over the A-frame while Beau is watching. Someday you may return the favor. Dogs react to different obstacles in different ways, and Beau may be hesitant of heights but terrific in tunnels.

Progressing at Your Own Pace

Once Beau is comfortable on a low A-frame, begin raising it very gradually. Slow is the way to go when teaching an obstacle. There are two main elements to a perfect performance on the A-frame: touching the contact zones and using the rear legs for propulsion on the way up. It's easiest for Beau to perfect these elements when the height is raised in small increments. He needs a chance to practice many times at each progressive height before the obstacle is made steeper.

Don't worry if the other dogs in your class climb the obstacle at full height before Beau does. When dogs are rushed on the A-frame they often start leaping on and off, missing the vital contact zones. Then they have to be retrained—a much slower process than getting it right the first time. The secret to achieving long-term accuracy in the shortest possible time is to

WHAT YOU NEED WHEN INTRODUCING YOUR DOG TO THE OBSTACLES

For Your Dog

- Flat buckle collar of leather or nylon

- Leather or nylon lead (leash), four to six feet long, preferably with the loop removed so it won't get caught on the equipment

- A six- to 12-inch piece of leather, nylon or clothesline rope with a snap attached to the end to make a miniature loopless lead (this is called a tab in agility and obedience jargon)

- Favorite toys and treats (also known as lures)

- An upbeat attitude, with the three *P*'s: pats, praise and patience

For You

- Comfortable shoes with sufficient support and traction

- Comfortable, older clothes

- No jewelry or belts that dangle or jangle

- A sense of humor

For Both of You

- Safe, secure obstacles set as low as they go

- Help from a good instructor, if possible

make slow but steady progress, without having to go back and correct bad habits.

For Safety's Sake

An A-frame made to accommodate novice dogs working at different heights must be strongly supported or it could collapse under a dog's weight. Always check the sturdiness of any A-frame Beau will be practicing on before he climbs it.

NAME THAT OBSTACLE

When you introduce Beau to an obstacle, give it a name. Then use that name, and only that name, every time you work that obstacle. For example, you might call the A-frame "A" or "Climb" and the dog walk "Walk," "Plank" or "Ramp." It doesn't matter what you name an obstacle, as long as the name is short and easy to remember under pressure. The name will become Beau's cue or command to head for a particular obstacle, and he will soon learn to discriminate between them.

Cross-Over (a.k.a. Cross Walk or Dog Cross)

The cross-over is four inclined planks, each 12 feet long, meeting at an elevated platform. From above, it looks like an X with a table top in the middle.

So many possibilities, but only one is correct. To conquer the cross-over, Beau will go up the correct plank (the one indicated by the judge's course design) on your command and/or signal. You'll know which plank is correct and will begin indicating it to Beau as soon as he completes the previous obstacle, so ascending is usually the easy part. But coming down can be a challenge. Beau will descend by either the left, right or middle plank, also as indicated on the course design, but you'll have less time to cue him. Points are lost for ascending or descending the wrong plank and for missing the yard-long contact zones at the bottom of each plank.

Stepping Off on the Right Paw

If you chose a form of agility that uses the cross-over, introduce it after the A-frame and before the dog walk. If the cross-over is not required by your agility organization, keep reading anyway, as the preliminary training for the cross-over and the dog walk is exactly the same, and every organization uses the dog walk.

Are you training on adjustable obstacles? Lucky you. Lay the cross-over nearly flat on the ground and remove two planks so Beau can go across in a straight line (if training on the dog walk, simply lay it nearly flat but don't remove any boards).

If you don't have adjustable obstacles, introduce Beau to a raised practice plank—a sturdy board about 12 inches wide and between four and six feet long. The plank should have a nonslip surface and can be held off the ground by cement blocks.

Whether you use an adjustable cross-over or dog walk or a practice plank, you'll need a helper ("spotter" in agility jargon). The spotter will walk on one side of Beau while you steady him from the other side. That will help Beau feel secure and keep him safe while he learns to keep all four feet on the board and go from one end to the other without jumping off.

Help Beau across the lowered obstacle or practice plank by starting about six feet from it with his nose aimed toward the middle of the board. Then guide him across with one hand holding his collar. Use your other hand to encourage him to look down at the plank while moving forward. If Beau has trouble keeping his back feet on the board, steady him by placing your free hand on his hip. Then your spotter can keep Beau focused and moving forward by gently tapping the board several inches in front of Beau's nose and offering an occasional treat.

As Beau becomes confident on the lowered obstacle, begin raising it gradually. If you don't have adjustable obstacles, wean Beau off the practice plank by placing him (if you're able to lift him) on the descending plank of the regulation height cross-over or dog walk. Then encourage him to walk down to the ground. After he does it several times, try the obstacle from beginning to end. If you can't lift Beau, take him from the practice plank directly to the regulation cross-over or dog walk and guide him up, across and down. Be sure to bring your spotter along.

Once Beau is working on the actual cross-over or dog walk, familiarize him with its name by calling it "walk," "plank," or whatever name you chose every time he approaches it. It's okay to call the cross-over and the dog walk by the same name, as they appear similar from a dog's-eye view.

No matter which method you use, Beau could get nervous or curious as the obstacle becomes higher, and may stop to get his bearings or view the scenery from the top. Let him. Wait several seconds, then entice him to finish walking across. Continue using a spotter every time Beau is on the practice plank or the dog walk until he is consistently sure-footed and confident.

Progressing at Your Own Pace

After Beau performs the cross-over easily at full height in a straight line and no longer needs your steadying hand on his collar, it's time to add the other

BACK-CHAINING

Adjustable contact obstacles are a rather new concept and not everyone is lucky enough to have them. Thousands of dogs have earned agility titles by learning on regulation height obstacles and Beau can, too—although, depending on his size, you may call the technique "back-straining" instead of "back-chaining."

The method is the same for every contact obstacle, so I'll use the A-frame as an example. All it involves is lifting Beau and placing him a few feet up the ramp, on-lead, facing down. Then walk him down the ramp and praise him. If he's a little guy, keep lifting him higher until he's walking down from as high as you can place him up there (with a spotter on the other side of him, of course). Later, when you take him to the other side of the A-frame and entice him up, he'll already be familiar with the view from the top and know how to come down.

Back-chaining also works with sequences (see Chapter 4). If Beau seems reluctant to complete a sequence, he may be unsure of the last or next-to-last obstacle in the series. Practice the last obstacle first, then the next-to-last, and so on all the way back to the first. Then, when you try them in order, they will all be familiar.

two planks and pay attention to the contact zones (see "Concentrating on Contact Zones," later in this chapter). With a spotter on each side of Beau, give the command that sends him up the cross-over. While he climbs, position yourself by the contact zone of the plank on the right. Just before Beau reaches the top, call him down the right side plank. Clapping and verbal encouragement usually work, but if Beau already knows the command "right," this is the time to use it (see "Obedience for Agility Dogs" in Chapter 4 for more on some basic commands your dog should know). If Beau seems confused, help him down the right plank with your hand on his collar. Whether he reaches the bottom alone or with your help, praise him profusely. Once he begins to understand this obstacle, use different planks for the ascent.

Teach the left board exactly the same way, but expect it to take a little longer if Beau was previously trained in formal obedience. Since you will be calling him from beside the contact zone of the left plank, he will be on your right side. This may make him a bit hesitant at first if he is only used to working off your left side.

The straight path should be the easy course, right? Wrong. It's the toughest for most dogs and handlers, for two reasons. First, being able to command Beau to "wait" or even "down" on the platform is practically a prerequisite (see Chapter 4), and second, you will have to make an agile move, too.

Send Beau up one of the planks and give the "wait" or the "down" command just before or just as he reaches the platform (both the command and how soon you give it depend upon your dog's speed). The object is to have Beau slow down, stop or lie down as soon as he reaches the platform because you need time to reach the center plank and signal the descent. If Beau is over-eager and iffy on the stay, ask a helper to keep him in position while you make your move.

You have a choice of routes when rushing to reach the contact zone area of the center plank. Either duck under the right side plank (careful of your head), or go around the right plank (oops—don't trip over it!). Now call Beau down to you, slowing him with your hand on his collar to help him make contact with the crucial zone. All done? Whew! Beau deserves lots of praise. Okay, so do you.

Duchess, owned by Marilyn Bain (facing camera), gets encouragement on the dog walk from her owner and Jean Carter, who serves as spotter.

Duchess has become confident enough to cross the dog walk without help.

Eventually you will perform the straight course by sending Beau up the plank while you head for the contact zone and give the "wait" or "down" command on the move. But there's no need to rush it. Use spotters as long as you need to and take time to steady Beau's "wait" or "down-stay" on the platform until he becomes reliable. Meanwhile, practice arriving at the obstacle from gentle angles, always straightening your approach a few feet before Beau mounts the plank. Decide ahead which planks you will have Beau ascend and descend and stick with your plan. If Beau has trouble straightening his body after approaching any contact obstacle from an angle, place orange road safety pylons in front of the obstacle in the shape of a funnel. That should help him straighten his approach so he begins with all four feet solidly on the plank.

For Safety's Sake

Use only a buckle collar when teaching the cross-over and the dog walk. If Beau wears a leash or tab, he could step on it and lose his balance.

To keep Beau from jumping or falling off the cross-over, dog walk or even the practice plank, use an alert spotter until Beau gains control of his hind end and consistently keeps all four feet on the boards.

Marilyn gets Duchess used to being handled from either side right from the beginning.

Don't let Beau race across the cross-over or the dog walk before he walks them several times. Some dogs rush across these obstacles at first out of fear. There will be plenty of time to gain speed after Beau learns to love walking the planks.

Dog Walk

Even though the dog walk is really a cat walk, Beau will prance across it with pride once he feels secure on it. It's made of three long, narrow planks. One is inclined for ascending, another is straight across and resembles a balance beam, and the third is inclined for descending. The bottom few feet of the inclined planks are contact zones.

Beau will demonstrate his deftness on the dog walk by going up the ramp on your command or signal, confidently crossing the long plank and descending smoothly, without missing a contact zone.

Stepping Off on the Right Paw

Please refer to this section under "Cross-Over," on pages 26–27.

Progressing at Your Own Pace

Work Beau on either side of you and encourage him to move out ahead of you as his performance improves. Then begin approaching the obstacle from various angles. As Beau gains speed, it may be necessary to place orange safety pylons in front of the obstacle in a funnel shape to help him straighten his body before he steps on the plank.

The easier the dog walk becomes, the faster Beau will go, and one day he will probably skip a contact zone. Once is enough, or missing contact zones could become a habit. To help you keep Beau's toes within the zones, see "Concentrating on Contact Zones," later in this chapter.

For Safety's Sake

The safety considerations are the same as for the cross-over, above. Please don't skip them.

See-Saw (a.k.a. Teeter-Totter)

The see-saw looks like the one you used to play on, minus the handles, which would only trip your dog. But to Beau it looks like another dog walk, except, surprise—it moves! Because it has the added challenge of movement, the see-saw is a complicated contact obstacle and should be the last one taught (or next to last if you plan to do UKC agility and use the sway bridge).

Beau will successfully play see-saw by mounting the obstacle from the designated side on your signal, making it pivot downward, descending after the plank touches the ground, and touching the contact zones on his way up and down.

Stepping Off on the Right Paw

With a spotter on one side of Beau and you on the other, put your hand on his collar and walk him up the plank, stopping just at the middle. Use your free hand to keep the plank from falling too fast and edge Beau forward inch by inch until the plank starts downward. Then tell Beau to wait (use the "wait" command whether he already knows it or not) while you gently lower the plank until it reaches the ground. Walk Beau slowly down and off the plank and let him know what a fine fellow he is.

If Beau is frightened by the movement, or if he is an exceptionally large dog, enlist a second helper to control the plank so both you and your spotter have both hands free to steady Beau.

Proceeding at Your Own Pace

As Beau gains confidence on the see-saw, let him, not you, make the board pivot. But always have him wait at the top until the board touches the ground.

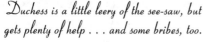

Duchess is a little leery of the see-saw, but gets plenty of help . . . and some bribes, too.

She did the see-saw. Yea, Duchess!

That little stop at the top has to become a habit, as dogs lose points in competition for reaching the ground before the see-saw does. The mistake is called a "fly-off" in agility jargon.

When the see-saw becomes a breeze for Beau, approach it from gradual angles and practice it with you on either side of him. Straighten his approach with your orange funnel, if necessary.

For Safety's Sake

During early training, always control the board or ask someone to help you with it. Never allow it to crash to the ground, and always wait for it to stop vibrating before bringing Beau down.

Do whatever it takes to keep Beau from jumping or falling off the obstacle, even if it means holding him on it in a comforting bear hug. If Beau is a big boy, ask for all the helpers you need. Later will be payback time, so make yourself available when your helpers need help.

Sway Bridge

Did you ever see a Western movie where a bridge made of rope and wooden planks sways precariously over a ravine? That's the prototype of the UKC's sway bridge. But don't worry. The one Beau will cross is only 18 inches high, has ramps and contact zones for ascending and descending, and limited movement for safety.

Beau will conquer the sway bridge by touching the contact zone during his ascent, moving across the swaying section with careful concentration and touching the contact zone on descent. When navigating the swaying portion (the bridge), he is required to place all four feet on the planks individually, not leap across.

Stepping Off on the Right Paw

Beau will welcome your steadying hand on his collar when he is introduced to this obstacle. Use a spotter to keep him from trying to jump off when he first feels movement beneath his feet, and another helper to stabilize the bridge, so it sways only slightly while Beau gets used to it. Your helper should let the bridge move a little more when Beau's body language says he is ready to handle it.

Little dogs won't make the bridge move much, but mastering this obstacle may take longer if Beau is a big boy, because every shift of weight adds to the swing. Be patient, and generous with praise and bribes. Taking a treat out of your lowered hand (so low it touches the bridge) every few steps will give Beau reason to keep going and help him focus on his footing.

When Beau crosses the bridge smoothly and confidently without anyone stabilizing it, remove your hand from his collar. Continue using a spotter until there is no doubt of Beau's good intentions when he mounts the obstacle, and treat his every crossing like an occasion.

Progressing at Your Own Pace

With most agility obstacles, you will gradually work toward gaining some speed. Not so with the sway bridge. Beau will do best on this obstacle if he shows an understanding of how it works by moving slowly and smoothly enough to keep the bridge steady. Make use of the command "easy," whether Beau knows what it means or not. Saying it frequently, while using your hands to slow and steady him, will teach him its meaning soon enough. Later it will be a big help, especially if Beau tends be quick on the course.

Work on approaching the sway bridge from various angles with you on either side of Beau, and teach him to stop and wait for it to stabilize if he inadvertently makes it move too much.

For Safety's Sake

If there is any question in your mind about whether or not Beau still needs a spotter, he does. When he is completely comfortable and totally committed to the obstacle, you'll know it.

Swing Plank

Four feet long and 20 inches wide, the UKC's swing plank has a chain at each end holding it three inches above the ground. It's free to swing horizontally in all directions, but not far enough or fast enough to put Beau in danger. Although this is a plank obstacle, it's low enough not to need ramps or contact zones.

Beau will succeed at the swing plank if he mounts it from the designated end, steps on it with all four feet while moving across it confidently and exits gently at the opposite end, without making it jerk backward. Top performers cross it briskly while hardly making it move at all.

Stepping Off on the Right Paw

Teach Beau the sway bridge before trying the swing plank. He should be relaxed on the bridge (but doesn't have to be perfect) before trying the plank.

A solid introduction and plenty of experience are the keys to a fine performance on the swing plank. Start with a spotter to help steady Beau and a second helper to stabilize the obstacle. Walk Beau up to the plank with your reassuring hand on his collar (you'll have to take it off for an instant to avoid bumping the chain with your arm). By the time you get to this advanced obstacle, Beau will know you want him to mount it, but be prepared for initial reluctance when he feels the plank move beneath his front feet. That's when your helper should use his or her foot to gradually stabilize the obstacle.

You and your spotter should do whatever it takes to keep Beau from jumping off, including hugs, treats and anything else you did to help him gain confidence on the sway bridge. Use the command "easy" when Beau mounts and dismounts and tell him to "wait" if he makes the plank move too much. Every time he tries to stabilize it himself, tell him what a good sport he is and soon he will like the swing plank. After all, kids learn to love sliding boards even though many of them cling to the top in terror the first time, eventually mustering the courage to let go and plunge into Mom or Dad's waiting arms.

CONCENTRATING ON CONTACT ZONES

When Beau learns to love walking the planks, he may start leaping eagerly on the contact obstacles and racing up, across and down. While that's a great agility attitude, it could cause contact zone problems unless you are prepared to prevent them. Missed contact zones are seldom a problem while dogs are learning an obstacle, so handlers are often caught off guard when their dog becomes proficient, speeds up and starts missing contact zones. Don't let missed zones become a habit. It's easier to teach Beau to touch every contact zone right from the start than to give him too much freedom and try to correct habitual misses later.

There are several ways to teach dogs to touch contact zones. One way is to use the word "easy" (see "Obedience for Agility Dogs," in the next chapter). Even if Beau doesn't know what "easy" means, say it every time you see him approaching a contact obstacle too fast, and repeat it when he is on the way down if you need to. Combined with your body language or your helpful hands slowing him down, he'll soon learn it.

Did you ever do the limbo? It's a Caribbean dance where each dancer in turn bends backward and tries to go under the limbo stick without touching it or falling down. The stick is held progressively lower until only one dancer is left. No, we're not going to make Beau bend over backwards, but you can use your arm like a limbo stick. Just hold it straight out over the plank so Beau has to duck under it (just a little) to ascend the obstacle. Then do the same on the down side. Doing the limbo should slow Beau just enough so that he will touch the contact zones. Use your other arm, if necessary, to keep him from jumping the limbo stick instead of ducking under it.

If Beau ascends reliably but descends so fast you're afraid he'll miss the contact zone, place your hand, holding a treat, on the grass or floor just in front of the descent ramp. That will make him focus his eyes downward and keep his feet on the board. Don't raise your hand to give him the treat. Let him take it out of your hand on the ground.

There are many ways to prevent contact zone problems, and you will learn others if you attend agility classes. If Beau is active and medium to large in size, expect to spend some time concentrating on contact zones. Small dogs seldom miss contact zones, although there are always exceptions.

If Beau is nervous about the swing plank, his body tension or outright case of the shakes will make the obstacle swing more than it should. Experience and confidence will help, and soon Beau will learn where to place his feet to cross with maximum speed and minimum motion. Pay particular attention to Beau's dismount. Ideally he should exit the plank at the same smooth pace he crossed it, one foot at a time, without hopping or jumping.

Because their body weight causes only slight movement, little dogs have the advantage on the swing plank, just as they did on the sway bridge. But that doesn't hurt Beau the Boxer's chance to win his class. After all, dogs compete against similar size dogs in agility.

Progressing at Your Own Pace

When Beau makes smooth crossings so consistently that your spotter and your plank stabilizer are both snoozing and you haven't had to touch his collar in ages, let your friends go back to their own dogs. Now try angled entrances, keeping the angles even slighter than usual at first. It's easy for dogs to step on the plank sideways, missing the entrance entirely, but it's best if Beau never realizes that. Chances are he won't, if you always plan your route so he has enough time and space to straighten his body before stepping onto the swing plank.

For Safety's Sake

With the plank only three inches off the ground, there isn't much chance of Beau hurting himself, even as the result of an unintentional dismount. But you could bruise yourself. Be careful not to bang your hand or arm on the chain while helping Beau mount. It won't feel good, and Beau won't like it either because the plank will jerk.

TUNNEL TIME

Dogs and spectators both find the tunnels especially entertaining, and agility gives them four types of tunnel fun: the open or pipe tunnel, the closed or collapsed tunnel (used by every agility organization) and the hoop and crawl tunnels, unique to the UKC. Most handlers begin tunnel training with the open tunnel.

Open or Pipe Tunnel

The open or pipe tunnel is a flexible open tube approximately 15 feet long. Its height and width are both approximately 24 inches. At agility trials it

Jean steadies Duchess on one side of a miniature pipe tunnel while Marilyn calls her dog and guides her through on-lead.

may be bent at right angles, formed into a U-turn or presented in any variety of curves. That means Beau will not be able to see the exit from the entrance.

All Beau has to do to be terrific on this tunnel is enter the end designated by the judge's course design, go directly through and exit at the other end.

Stepping Off on the Right Paw

If temporarily compressing a regulation open tunnel to a shorter length is an option, start with the tunnel between three and four feet long in a straight line. Otherwise, create a practice tunnel from a plastic or cardboard industrial-size drum, or remove the bottom from an aging, but clean, plastic garbage pail.

Attach a six-foot or longer lead to Beau's buckle collar and introduce him to the tunnel or drum by letting him examine (read "sniff") both ends of it. Then, depending upon his size, have him sit or lie down at one end (his eyes should be at a level where he can see through the tunnel). Ask a helper to hold Beau's lead while you walk to the other end of the tunnel, then hand the lead to you through the tunnel. If Beau hasn't learned to stay yet, your

Duchess is ready for a run-by.

39

helper can keep him in place with a hand on his collar. After you have the lead in hand, step back a foot or two from the tunnel's exit to give Beau room to come through. Ready? Kneel down so you can look through the opening at Beau and call him happily, using whatever word you choose to designate this tunnel. As you call, your helper should release Beau's collar. When he comes through, make him glad he did.

If Beau hesitates, clapping or opening your arms for a hug may convince him to come through the tunnel. Another motivator is letting him see you place a treat on the ground just past the exit. But putting food inside the tunnel is a no-no, as it will teach Beau to stop and sniff the floor of the tunnel. If positive persuasion doesn't work, extend your arm (the one holding the lead) into the tunnel and use the lead to guide Beau through.

After Beau eagerly bounds through the drum, barrel or shortened tunnel several times, he'll be ready for "run-bys." In agility jargon, run-bys are what you do while your dog performs the obstacle. With Beau beside you on a loopless tab, walk toward the practice tunnel and stop six to eight feet from it. Encourage Beau to look toward the obstacle, then head for it briskly and give the verbal tunnel command and a hand signal as you reach the opening. Drop the tab as Beau dives in, run by the obstacle and meet him at the other end for a celebration. Now try run-bys with Beau on your other side.

After Beau is successful with three or four run-bys in a row, move on to the regulation length tunnel and remove the tab. With the full-length tunnel laid out in a straight line (so he can see through it), place Beau on a sit or down on one side of the tunnel and have a helper hold his collar while you go to the other end.

Then call him through, just as you did with the practice tunnel. When Beau is confident with the full-size tunnel, attach his tab and do run-bys, using your tunnel command and a hand signal (the signal can be as simple as a directional gesture toward the entrance), with Beau on either side of you. Reward every good try with praise and play.

Progressing at Your Own Pace

When run-bys become easy, begin bending the tunnel a little bit at a time; sometimes to the right and other times to the left. Make sure Beau can still see the light at the end of the tunnel the first few times. After that, bend the tunnel a little more during every practice session, as long as Beau continues to come though easily. If he ever hesitates, give him easier angles so he can

PUSHING BEAU'S BUTTONS

Throughout this book I've been reminding you to pet and praise Beau often as he tries new agility moves and perfects old ones. But petting and praise only work when it's sincere and maybe a little silly—okay, good and silly. Praising your dog in a drab monotone won't mean much to him, even if you mean every word of it. In fact, he'll soon tune you out and start sniffing around for something more interesting.

How can you make the praise so powerful that Beau wants more? Most dogs love drama. "Way to go, Beau!" "All *Riiight!*" "Yeehaw!" Find the happy words that come naturally to you and use them in an excited, cheerful voice whenever Beau does something right. Dance with him. Hug him. Give him a treat. Next time give him a different treat. Play wrestle. Throw a toy. He'll never know what's going to happen when he does something right, but he'll sure want to find out.

Soon you'll know which words make his tail thump. Which treat is his favorite. Whether he wants to retrieve or play tug with his toy. Those are his buttons. Beau's buttons are what turn him on and tune him in more than anything else. Pushing them makes him happy, and when he's happy he's willing to try again, try harder, get it right. And that makes you happy, too.

see a little light at the other end, before trying more severe curves again. Take your time. What you are building is Beau's faith. He has to believe there will be light, and you, at the other end of the tunnel.

Eventually you will bend the tunnel so it makes a right angle. Practice with this 90-degree angle in both directions and finally add a U-turn and S-curves to Beau's repertoire. Always take your time and make time for praise and play. Instilling confidence in Beau is more important than rushing into tight turns.

Once Beau bounces through tunnels of every imaginable configuration, gradually work on sending him through the tunnel ahead of you. Occasionally placing a treat a few feet from the exit will make Beau even more eager to bound through. When he has mastered entering the tunnel ahead of you on command, begin work on angled approaches. As always, start with easy angles and increase the difficulty as Beau becomes ready. When sending him ahead of you or teaching angled approaches, the fastest way to make progress is to go back to an easier lesson right away if Beau seems confused or misses the tunnel entrance. Continuous small successes are what it takes to create a confident agility dog.

For Safety's Sake

When sharing equipment with an agility club or class, be careful not to send Beau into one end of the tunnel at the same time another dog dashes into the opposite end.

Closed or Collapsed Tunnel

The closed or collapsed tunnel has a rigid entrance between two and three feet long with a height and width of around 24 inches, similar in diameter to the pipe tunnel. But the resemblance ends at the entrance. The rest of the closed tunnel is a chute made of lightweight fabric that lays flat on the ground and extends 12 to 15 feet. The closed tunnel is a real crowd pleaser. Watching it is like seeing a dog scamper through a burrow, but better, because the dog's entire outline can be seen as it races through.

Beau will conquer the closed tunnel by entering at the entrance on your command, and exiting through the chute.

Stepping Off on the Right Paw

Teach the closed tunnel only after Beau happily handles 90-degree angles and U-turns in the open tunnel. That way he will be used to finding his way through an obstacle's dark interior. Angled approaches and sending him to the open tunnel ahead of you are not prerequisites to learning the closed tunnel. Beau can continue working on various approaches after he is confident inside both tunnels.

Introduce Beau to a smaller version of the closed tunnel by rolling back the fabric until the whole tunnel, entrance included, is about four feet long. Put Beau on a long lead and position him in either a sit or down just in front of the entrance (the opening should be at his eye level). Ask a helper to keep him in position while you go to the other end of the chute. Hold the chute open (but not off the ground) so Beau can see you, take the lead (through the tunnel) from your helper, and call your dog through with your closed tunnel command (it can be the same as your open tunnel command, if you like). Keep the chute open as Beau comes through and praise him when he reaches you.

After three or four successful repetitions, move on to run-bys. With the chute still short, Beau on-lead and your helper holding the chute open from the side (so Beau can't see him or her through the opening), head for the tunnel from several feet away. Give your tunnel command and hand signal and guide Beau into the opening, if necessary, before releasing the lead. Then run by the obstacle and meet and greet him on the other side. If this goes well, gradually work up to releasing Beau just at the entrance without guiding him in.

Beau may relate the closed tunnel to his open tunnel work and breeze through this introduction in no time. But don't worry if he does it in slow time. Is he hesitant about this tunnel? Then go back to standing in front of it, looking through and calling him a few more times. Greet him happily and try run-bys again after he seems comfortable with the tunnel.

As soon as you and Beau are happy with his run-bys, ask your helper to increase the length of the chute by three feet, while still holding it open so Beau can see light at the other end. After three or four successful run-bys, increase the length by another yard, then another. Chances are Beau won't treat it any differently. But if he does spook at any point along the way, ask your helper to roll the chute back a few feet until your dog's confidence returns.

Too much repetition will bore Beau, so even if he's doing great, stop after you accomplish run-bys at six or seven feet and wait for your next practice session to continue the progression. When Beau performs run-bys the full length of the regulation chute (which is still being held open by your helper), it's time to move on to the next step—lowering the chute.

Ask your helper to wait until Beau starts through the chute, then lower the fabric so it just brushes his back as he burrows along. Meet him with much praise. Next time have your helper lower the chute a bit more, so it rests on Beau's back. From then on, continue lowering it until Beau pushes through on his own from beginning to end. Way to go, Beau!

What if Beau progresses well for awhile and then becomes frightened? Just roll up the chute so he can see you at the other end and call him through for a petting party. Then gradually go back to having your helper lower the chute.

Progressing at Your Own Pace

After Beau perfects run-bys through a totally collapsed tunnel, begin handling him from either side of you. Then add angled approaches. Finally,

When Duchess is ready for the full-length closed tunnel, Jean steadies her while Marilyn looks through the tunnel and calls her dog.

Duchess earns a hug!

RAIN, RAIN, COME TODAY!

The collapsed tunnel won't be your only problem on a soggy agility course, so if you plan to compete outdoors—and you'll limit the number of events you can attend if you don't—put on a slicker and practice in the rain sometimes. Don't be surprised if Beau needs a reminder before he lies down on a water-logged pause table, and be sure to tell him what a brave boy he is when he complies. The first few times you practice on wet grass, go slower than normal, wear shoes that keep you from sliding and be sure Beau touches every contact zone.

Not every agility dog is trained to be reliable on a wet course, so if Beau is, he'll have a competitive advantage. Maybe you'll even find yourself saying, "Rain, rain, come today. Beau and I know how to play."

teach Beau to run out ahead of you and duck into the tunnel from either a straight approach or a slight angle. Again, an occasional treat or favorite toy waiting by the exit will be a good incentive. Just don't let him have it if he tries to run around the tunnel instead of going through it.

Since working several feet in front of you and approaching obstacles from an angle are an important part of successful agility work, Beau will put the finesse on each obstacle by perfecting his approaches. They will become a little easier with every obstacle.

To paraphrase the old saying, into every agility career a little rain will fall. Yes, it may rain the day of the agility trial, and the closed tunnel, not to mention the whole course, may be wet. Some dogs won't mind a bit, but others will consider pushing their way through water-logged fabric a major inconvenience. Prepare for the possibility during practice (after Beau has learned to love the full-length tunnel) by using a spray bottle to dampen the fabric just a little, and gradually work up to soaking the chute. Is Beau a little bit of a dog? Then wet chutes are heavier and harder for him to push his way through, and he deserves extra praise.

If Beau refuses to burrow through a wet tunnel, put him back on-lead, enlist a helper, shorten the wet chute and go back to square one. With your helper holding Beau, stand at the other end of the shortened chute, hold it open, call Beau to you and use the lead to guide him through. Don't hesitate to bribe him with praise and his favorite goodies. Progress to run-bys, with your helper gradually letting out a few more feet of soggy chute and laying it lower until Beau learns that dogs don't melt in the rain.

For Safety's Sake

When you were a youngster, were you ever short-sheeted at camp or a sleeping party? Did it make you wary the next time you got into bed? That's what a tangled chute could do to Beau. Prevention is the best cure, so always check to make sure the chute is tangle-free before sending Beau through. If he ever becomes entangled anyway, help him find his way out, praise him without pampering him, and restore his confidence in the obstacle by immediately sending him through a shortened, open-ended version.

As much as you want to give Beau verbal encouragement, keep quiet when he is in the tunnel. If you cheer him on while you are running by the tunnel, he may veer toward the sound of your voice and end up turned around or tangled. Save the praise until you meet him at the exit, then be sure to let him have it. "Yay, Beau!"

Hoop Tunnel

The hoop tunnel is comprised of eight hoops no more than an inch off the ground. Each one is about 30 inches in diameter (although they may be a bit bigger if traditional hula hoops are used). The hoops are set in a frame at a 60-degree angle to each other. Simply put, that means there is plenty of space between the hoops for a less than thoroughly trained dog to slip out of the obstacle. Unlike the open and collapsed tunnels, Beau will be able to see you the whole time he is in the hoop tunnel.

All Beau has to do in the hoop tunnel is enter at the entrance, go all the way through, and exit at the exit. But that may not be as easy as it sounds. The most common faults made on this tunnel are entering or exiting from the side (between the hoops) instead of through the entrance and exit.

Stepping Off on the Right Paw

Put a long lead or line on Beau to introduce him to the hoop tunnel. Then leave him with a helper at one end of the tunnel while you go to the other end. Take the lead through the tunnel from your helper (you'll have to reach in to get it). When you are ready, look at Beau through the hoops, encourage him to come to you, and go hand over hand on the lead while backing up slightly as he gets closer. That keeps the slack out of the lead without putting any pressure on it. Try to make sure there is no slack so you can use the lead to straighten Beau if he tries to exit between the hoops, but don't make it tight enough to interfere if he continues through the tunnel correctly.

Fancee, owned by Vel and Charles "Bud" Kramer, demonstrates her expertise in the hoop tunnel.

At first he may go slower than you expect. Even though the hoops are only an inch off the ground, he still has to adjust his footwork to keep from touching them.

When Beau performs the hoop tunnel well on-lead, remove the lead and ask your helper to hold him at one end until you call. Then back up with your arms wide, encouraging Beau to come through for a big bear hug. If he exits between the hoops, don't make a big deal of it. Just put him back on-lead for a little more practice.

When Beau comes barreling straight through every time, it's time to try run-bys without a helper. Approach the entrance with your hand on Beau's collar and send him through. When running by, stay close to the hoops at first. Going wide would tempt Beau to exit between the hoops and join you way out yonder. Be sure to practice on both sides.

Progressing at Your Own Pace

Once your run-bys flow easily, begin angled approaches from either side at a very slight angle. As your angles gradually become more challenging, be aware of where Beau's body is in relation to the entrance. He needs enough room to straighten out or you may inadvertently encourage him to dive in from the side. Be unpredictable when you meet Beau at the other end, so he never knows if the course continues straight ahead or makes a left or right turn after he exits.

For Safety's Sake

Never let Beau drag a lead, especially one with a loop, through the hoop tunnel. It could get caught on one of the hoops. While that is hardly dangerous, it would give him quite a jerk. In fact, it would feel just like an obedience correction, and could really confuse Beau because he was doing something right when it happened.

Crawl Tunnel

The crawl tunnel is similar to the hoop tunnel in two ways: Beau will be able to see you while he is in it, and the supports are widely spaced so he could make the mistake of entering or exiting along the side of the obstacle. The singular characteristic of the crawl tunnel is that it will be lower than Beau is tall, so he will have to crawl through it. The crawl tunnel is adjustable to a variety of heights, so the amount of crawl space corresponds to the size of the dog using it. It is between five and six feet long and its ceiling is covered with cloth.

Beau will conquer the crawl tunnel by dropping down and entering at the entrance without hesitation, crawling through and exiting at the end.

Stepping Off on the Right Paw

Follow the steps used when training the hoop tunnel, with one exception. Begin by adjusting the height of the crawl space so it is just above Beau's head and he can go through without crawling. (This may be impossible if Beau is a Great Dane and the tunnel can't be adjusted higher than maximum competition height.) Then attach a long lead, enlist a helper and follow the steps you used to teach Beau the hoop tunnel.

After a few successful tries, lower the tunnel. If you can lower it in small increments, do so. If not, lower it to Beau's regulation height, get waaaay down, look at him through the tunnel and cheer him on as he figures out how to stay inside the obstacle and come to you. Did Beau lower his body and crawl through? Stage a short celebration. Then continue as you did with the hoop tunnel by calling Beau through off-lead, and finally freeing your helper and practicing run-bys from either side.

Oops! Did Beau hesitate at the entrance or try to leave through the side? Put the lead back on, lie down on your belly just outside the exit and stretch one arm through with a treat in your hand and your hand on the ground. The other hand holds the lead. As Beau moves toward you, gradually pull the treat toward you, always keeping it low. You won't be able to use both hands to take up the slack in the lead, but you can roll it over your free hand as he crawls closer. As soon as Beau understands the game, wait at the exit, keep your hands out of the tunnel and give him the treat just as he exits. When that goes well, try run-bys again.

Does your agility group have a crawl tunnel that is both length and height adjustable? If so, training Beau will be even easier. Begin by setting it between two and three feet long and just higher than Beau's head, then gradually lengthen and lower it, proceeding through the same training steps you used on the hoop tunnel.

Still having problems? Turn the crawl tunnel into a closed tunnel by draping cloth down both sides. Beau already knows how to do the closed tunnel, so after several sessions he should understand that walls with spaces are still barriers.

If Oliver the Great Dane can get through the crawl tunnel, any dog can. Oliver belongs to Bonnie Drabek.

Progressing at Your Own Pace

After Beau performs run-bys with little or no hesitation at the tunnel entrance, with you on either side of him, begin angled entrances. Gradually increase the angle and make sure Beau has enough time to straighten his body, just as you did when teaching the hoop tunnel.

For Safety's Sake

If Beau has some size to him and stands up inside the crawl tunnel, chances are the obstacle will lift up or even roll over. While it is lightweight and won't hurt him, it could scare him. By the time Beau is advanced enough to need the crawl tunnel in his repertoire, he'll know how to come when called and lie down from a distance, but refresh his memory on those commands before practicing this obstacle off-lead. Then, if he spooks and takes off because he overturned the tunnel, you'll be able to stop him.

WEAVE POLE CONTROL

The weave poles are a straight line of six to twelve poles, each about 36 inches tall and uniformly spaced about 24 inches apart. They flex at the base to accommodate large dogs and are painted for easy visibility.

Beau will whiz through the weave poles by always entering the obstacle from right to left, so the first pole is on his left side. Then he will weave so as to pass the second pole on his right side, the third pole on his left and so on, continuing this sequence until he exits the obstacle after the last pole.

One of the most spectacular of all agility obstacles, the weave poles are also the most difficult. Performed well, they demonstrate the epitome of control, flexibility and speed.

Stepping Off on the Right Paw

One method of teaching the weave poles is to use a chute that automatically guides Beau correctly through the obstacle. Used by many agility schools, these practice poles have heavy-gauge wire running from pole to pole in a U-shape so the chute looks like a continuous series of U's, half on one side and half on the other. When training Beau on this equipment, start with the chute wide enough so he can run through the center without turning at all. Put him on a sit-stay at the entrance (remember, the first pole must always be on his left), go to the other end, call him through using your weave command and reward him when he reaches you. If necessary, have a helper keep him in place until you call him. If he shows any tendency to exit between the

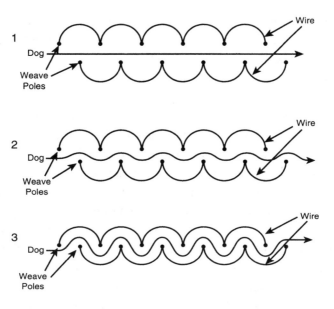

This is a diagram of a weave chute and how gradually closing it teaches a dog to weave.

poles, guide him through the chute on a long line until he understands what you want.

When Beau is comfortable with the chute, attach a loopless tab to his collar and perform the obstacle as a run-by. Holding the tab in your left hand with Beau on your left side, approach the entrance, give your weave command and signal and guide Beau in. Then drop the tab and run beside the chute as Beau runs through it. Meet him at the other end with praise, play or a treat. As soon as Beau understands what you want, remove the tab.

Gradually—very gradually—narrow the chute a little bit each week until the poles are in a straight line and Beau is weaving. Don't rush this step. Dogs do best when the chute is narrowed in small increments. It should take several weeks to go from running through a straight chute to weaving. Even after you reach that point, continue using the wire guides for several additional weeks. When you finally remove them, be prepared to correct any occasional missed pole immediately. If mistakes are more than occasional, put the wire guides back in place and use them for another month or more.

Another method of training the weave poles requires less equipment, but Beau will need more motivation. Start with only six poles. With Beau on your left side, attach a loopless tab to his collar and position yourself so you are facing the obstacle practically head on, but just a little to the right of the first pole. Hold the tab near the collar with your left hand, keeping your right hand free to direct Beau through the poles.

Begin by using your voice and body language to get him excited about playing the weaving game. Then give your weave command and signal, put your right hand in front of Beau at his eye level and step off with your left foot close to the first pole to start him (not you) weaving. From then on, keep him weaving all the way through. Use your right hand, as well as your foot work and body language, to indicate each change of direction, and your left hand on the tab to gently guide him. When it's obvious he understands, gradually add the rest of the poles, two at a time.

Weaving isn't part of natural dog play like jumping, climbing or burrowing, so it's up to you to make this obstacle fun. Always push the buttons that turn Beau on before you begin, and fuss over him when he exits. Unfortunately, some dogs get bored no matter how hard their owners try to make weaving wonderful. If Beau is one of them, wake him up with a treat in your right hand. He'll happily follow your hand as it snakes by the poles. Just don't reward him too soon. Beau earns the treat when he successfully exits the obstacle.

Motivating dogs through the weave poles without a chute.

Unlike the obstacles that dogs understand easily, it takes a lot of repetition to teach the weave poles, no matter what method you use. Meanwhile, you're dealing with a double problem because lots of repetition does become boring, and bored dogs stop paying attention and take even longer to learn. So what's the solution?

Even if you have no other practice-sized obstacles at home, a small, handy set of weave poles could change weaving from work to fun. Six dowels, mounted 20 to 24 inches apart on a base and standing only two feet high, make a super practice model. With the poles handy at home, Beau can get his repetition in frequent small doses, rather than a long drill once a week. Play the weaving game before taking Beau for a walk, during television commercials, before feeding and whenever you feel like giving him some extra attention. Keep it short and happy (but correct), with lots of excitement before you start ("Wanna weave?") and after you finish ("Gooood dog. Here's a cookie!"), and Beau will soon believe he was born to boogie around the weave poles.

After many weeks of repetition, one day Beau will seem to know how to do the poles without your guidance. Remove the tab and try it. Stay beside him as usual, directing with your right hand and using some body language. If he has a successful run, try it minus the body language, cueing him with only the weave command and a little directional aid with your right hand.

From then on, work toward getting Beau to weave alone, with no directional help from you. In fact, stay a step or two in front of him to motivate him to weave faster. If he misses a pole, correct him immediately but don't make a big deal of it. Just slow down the next time and stay closer to him until he is reliable again. Then gradually increase your distance.

When will you know that Beau has become a weaving wizard? When you can sit him at one end of the obstacle, call him from the other end and watch him enter correctly and weave his way to you. Wow!

Progressing at Your Own Pace

Up until now, you should have practiced the poles by starting Beau in front of the obstacle and just a little to the right of the first pole. Once he's completely reliable, try a variety of approach angles. Gradually increase the difficulty until Beau enters correctly, even after approaching from the left. Now Beau's weaving is good enough for most agility trials.

Elizabeth Ridley's Border Terrier, Crackers, demonstrates the finished product.

During advanced competition, you can save time by sending Beau to the poles ahead of you, trusting him to enter correctly and weave his way through completely on his own. When introducing this impressive maneuver to Beau, use only half a dozen poles at first. Approach them and give your weave command as usual, then slow down. If Beau weaves on ahead, meet him at the other end with special praise. Then send him ahead of you a little sooner the next time, gradually increasing the distance between you and the poles.

If Beau stops or hesitates because you aren't beside him, catch up to him and urge him on through. Before trying the poles again, place a treat on the ground at the opposite end and ask a helper to guard it. Show Beau the treat, then go well back from the entrance and send Beau on ahead. If he skips the obstacle altogether or weaves incorrectly, your helper should pick up the treat so Beau isn't rewarded for a mistake. Start over, but send Beau ahead

OH NO! HE MADE A MISTAKE

Dogs (okay, people too) often make mistakes when they are learning. So what should you do when Beau makes an honest mistake, like missing a weave pole or ticking (touching) a jump? Should you harshly tell him "No!" so he realizes his mistake? No!

When teaching agility, use praise, treats and toys to motivate Beau. When he does something right, he's rewarded. When he does something wrong, he isn't rewarded. It's as simple as that.

Harsh words, force or punishment should never be part of agility training. When Beau makes a mistake, say nothing. Just return to the obstacle and go back a step in training. If Beau was off-lead and out in front of you when he made the mistake, repeat the obstacle as a run-by. If he goofed on a run-by, try the obstacle on-lead. Praise him when he gets it right and continue training as if nothing happened. After all, nothing out of the ordinary did.

from closer to the entrance. If he weaves correctly, your helper should clap and cheer him on as he emerges to eat his treat. When you no longer need a helper, stop placing a treat at the exit. Instead, use praise and play, and sometimes toss a treat after Beau exits successfully.

If becoming a top competitor is your goal, it pays to teach Beau to weave off your right side. Then you can use the "weave on right advantage" some advanced courses offer (when the poles are situated so they would be most efficiently handled off the handler's right). Change sides only after Beau weaves well enough to do it in his sleep and enters correctly a little ahead of you. Then send him to the poles in the usual way, but switch sides behind him after he starts through. If he gets confused, give him a directional cue with your hand. When Beau is comfortable with you changing sides, try approaching the obstacle with him on your right. Help him with your loopless tab, if necessary.

For Safety's Sake

Are you rather short or is Beau a small dog? When training the weave poles, you'll bump your arm a lot less if you use two-foot-tall poles instead of the regulation three-footers.

HAPPY HURDLING

Agility hurdles are jumps in an array of appealing shapes and decorative colors. They are fast and fun and dominate every agility course, because there are often as many as or more hurdles than all the other obstacles combined.

There are several size categories in agility competition, and Beau will compete with other dogs of similar size, all jumping hurdles of the same height and length. Some hurdles will test his ability to jump high and others will showcase long jumps, but each obstacle will be sized to fit him. Agility hurdles are painted for maximum visibility. Depending upon the organization, their width varies between three-and-a-half and five feet.

Guidelines and Steps for Teaching Hurdles

The following guidelines and steps apply to all types of hurdles.

- Start low and go slow. Measure Beau's leg from the floor to his elbow. Elbow height, give or take an inch, is the best place to begin when introducing a new hurdle.

- Walk Beau over to each new hurdle and let him examine it from all sides before jumping it.

Marilyn lets Duchess examine the new obstacle.

Marilyn and Duchess jump together.

- Choose a command such as "jump" or "hup" and use it for every hurdle. Some handlers teach their dogs a different name for every jump and manage to command "double," "bar," "triple" and "broad" while under the pressure of competition. It's admirable but unnecessary. Handlers who only have to remember the word "jump" are equally successful.

- Make jumping a game Beau's happy to play, not a job. Never drill your dog long enough to bore him.

Step 1   Put Beau on a loopless lead on your left side, about six to ten feet from the elbow-height jump. Use your voice and body language to get him enthused about the joys of jumping. Give your jump command and trot over the jump with him. Praise him and do it again. When he eagerly runs beside you and takes the jump, change hands and try it with him on your right.

Three times on each side is enough. If going over a hurdle with your dog is impossible for you, begin by calling him over a hurdle set between two walls (a hallway, for example), so he can't go around it to reach you.

Step 2   Remove the lead and put Beau on a sit-stay about eight feet from the hurdle. Walk around to the other side, position yourself rather close to the middle of the hurdle and call Beau to you using your jump command. As he runs toward the hurdle, back up, open your arms and hug him when he reaches you. If Beau isn't steady on a sit-stay, have a helper hold him until you call him over the jump.

Step 3 Do this step only if the sides of your practice jump are plain uprights. If the jump has wings (agility jargon for big, fancy sides), spend extra time on steps one and two and then skip to step four.

Introduce run-bys with Beau wearing his loopless lead and you holding it in your left hand. Starting well back from the hurdle, excite Beau, give the jump command and move with him toward the hurdle. When you reach it, send Beau over (you may give the jump command again and a directional hand signal) while you run by the side, as close to the hurdle as possible. Keep enough slack in the lead so you don't pull Beau off balance. As he lands, veer toward him and meet him with praise.

When Beau does run-bys well from your left side, try them from the right. Most dogs learn run-bys quickly. That's good, because the sooner you get Beau jumping off-lead, the better.

Step 4 As soon as Beau understands on-lead run-bys, do them off-lead from either side. So far, so good? Then start raising the jump height gradually (most instructors advise two inches per week). Keep the praise coming and occasionally (not all the time) toss a treat or favorite toy to Beau just as he lands. That will keep him jumping for joy.

What if Beau understands exactly what you want him to do right from the start and clears every jump with ease? Is he special? Can he start jumping

Jean releases Duchess as Marilyn calls her over the hurdle.

regulation height right away? Yes and no. Yes, he is special and no, he still should gain height gradually. Even though his mind and spirit are soaring, his muscles, tendons and ligaments need time to catch up.

If Beau hesitates or goes around a jump at any time along the way, don't be overly concerned. Just lower the hurdle and do a few run-bys on-lead with lots of praise. Is Beau happy again? Then remove the lead and progress a little slower than before, until Beau is comfy at regulation height. When you are satisfied with this step, introduce a new hurdle starting with Step 1. Don't wait to master Step 5. That's a skill you will practice throughout your agility career.

Step 5 After Beau does run-bys from either side of you easily with the jump at regulation height, practice sending him to the jump a little ahead of you. Also, work on approaching the hurdle from various angles. Start easy and add difficulty gradually, focusing on Beau taking the jump solidly from the middle, not skimming the edges.

Panel Jump or High (Vertical or Solid) Hurdle

The panel or solid hurdle looks like a solid wall to your dog, but is really a series of crossboards, each three to four inches wide, stacked on top of each other. Its sides may be plain uprights or decorative wings, and it usually has a bar resting across the top.

To perfect the panel, Beau will jump it in the direction indicated by the course design without ticking (touching) it or knocking down the top bar.

Stepping Off on the Right Paw

A panel or solid jump, without wings, is the ideal obstacle for introducing Beau to jumping. Its plainness makes it the easiest jump to learn, as there is no empty space below the top bar to tempt Beau to duck under and no wings to jump over by mistake.

Teach Beau the panel jump as described on pages 56 to 59.

Progressing at Your Own Pace

After Beau happily jumps his regulation height on a plain panel jump (Step 4), go back to Step 1 and introduce the winged panel jump. Spend extra time on Step 2 with the winged jump, then skip Step 3. If Beau doesn't thoroughly understand that the middle section is the hurdle, he may try to go over the wings so he can be closer to you when you do wide run-bys.

PANEL JUMPS WITH PIZZAZZ

When Beau is reliable on the panel jump with wings, he's three-quarters of the way to doing a variety of solid hurdles. That's because the concept of jumping a solid panel is the same for all of them. All that remains is introducing Beau to the new shape and letting him know you want him to jump it.

Examples of commonly used variations on the panel jump include the barrel, the picket fence, the lattice and the fan jump, but jumps may be as creative as the club members who build them—as long as they comply with the organization's regulations.

The barrel jump is made of stacked crossboards just like the panel jump, but has barrels for wings. The picket fence hurdle resembles a traditional picket fence, except the ends are rounded or flattened for safety. Lattice work is framed to form the crossboards and wings in the lattice jump, and the fan jump is simply stacked crossboards held in place by fan-shaped wings.

Teach new jumps one at a time, always lowering the jump to Beau's elbow height. Take him through Steps 1 and 2 in one session, if possible. When you reach Step 4 (skip Step 3 on these jumps, as they are all winged), stop after a few successes off-lead. Don't raise the jump the same day you introduce it, and start with it low the next time you practice. Then begin raising it slowly, as recommended.

You will find different shaped wings and other decorations dressing up panel or solid jumps at agility trials, but by then Beau should recognize a panel jump when he sees one. Feeling creative? Build your own unique panel jumps or change the look of the ones you practice on by draping jackets over the wings and putting hats on the uprights. The variety will keep Beau interested and get him used to jumping any solid jump you direct him to.

For Safety's Sake

Be careful when doing run-bys with winged jumps. Of course you want to watch Beau, but those wings will trip you if you forget to watch where you're going.

Single Bar Jump or Hurdle

Sometimes plain-sided, but most often winged, the single bar jump usually consists of two or three bars with space between them, supported by uprights. The top bar is set at Beau's regulation height. The word "single" actually refers to the jump's width or spread, but sometimes the hurdle will consist of only one bar set at the required height. This creates an additional challenge, because if Beau isn't trained to jump a single bar, he may run under it.

Beau's performance will be perfect if he approaches the jump from the indicated direction without hesitation and clears the top bar without ticking it or knocking it down.

Stepping Off on the Right Paw

Is Beau a big dog? Then introduce him to a single bar jump consisting of three or four bars, if one is available. Medium and small dogs do fine with two bars.

If you have the option, begin training the single bar jump on a hurdle with plain uprights, and introduce wings only after Beau perfects Step 4. Then go back to Step 1 with the winged version, repeating everything except the run-bys on-lead.

Progressing at Your Own Pace

It pays to prepare Beau for a single bar jump that has only the top bar. Begin with Step 1 and work your way through. Oops, did Beau duck under? Better now than at a trial. Get a couple of feet of chicken wire, form it into a roll and place it under the jump, making sure there are no sharp edges sticking up. Dogs hate walking on wire, so Beau will gladly go over the top. Take time to put the wire in place every time you practice with one bar for the next few months. It will save time in the long run, because Beau will become conditioned to jump the single bar.

For Safety's Sake

Again, watch out for those wings. Don't let them grab your ankle.

Rail Fence Hurdle

Made to simulate the type of fence you often find in a corral or pasture, the rail fence hurdle is actually made of lightweight PVC pipe (as are many agility obstacles). Beau will probably progress through the steps quickly, since the concept of this hurdle is similar to the single bar jump.

Look at the concentration and communication between Jamie Walters and her Border Collie, Annie, on this single bar jump.

Double Oxer (Double Bar Jump)

Imagine two single bar jumps, one behind the other, and you'll know what the double oxer looks like. Both top bars will be set at Beau's regulation height, and additional bars below will keep him from being tempted to duck under. The jump's width or spread will vary with the organization. At most, it will be approximately the same as the jump's height.

Beau will do fine on the double bar if he takes the jump in the indicated direction without hesitation, and clears the top two bars without touching them.

Stepping Off on the Right Paw

Introduce the double oxer by taking Beau through the steps with the jump height and spread both set at his elbow height. For example, if Beau's elbow is eight inches off the ground, set the jump at eight inches high and make the spread about eight inches wide. Use a plain-sided jump at first, unless only winged hurdles are available.

Is Beau getting enough length on this wider hurdle? If not, help him remember that there are two hurdles in a row by setting the first one lower than the second for your first few weeks of practice. In agility jargon that's called an ascending spread.

Progressing at Your Own Pace
When Beau does the double easily at regulation height with you on either side of him, make it look different by decorating its uprights or wings.

For Safety's Sake
Nothing new here, but a few old reminders are worth repeating. Wear shoes with good traction, practice on safe footing, never have Beau wear an obedience (choke-type) collar when doing agility, and, of course, watch out for those wings.

Triple Bar Jump
The triple bar jump is a series of three bars of ascending height. The third bar will be set at Beau's regulation height, and the other two bars will be under it. For example, if Beau's jump height is 20 inches, the first bar will be around 10 inches high, the second 15 inches and the third will be 20 inches. Width is also a consideration, as the bars are evenly spaced at a distance that makes this jump about as broad as it is tall.

Beau will be tops at the triple if he takes off from the low side with no hesitation and clears all three bars without ticking or knocking over any of them.

Stepping Off on the Right Paw
Set the third bar at Beau's elbow height, and the first two bars as steps leading up to it. Then make the width of the jump approximately the same as the height, and introduce the triple bar the same way as any other hurdle. While not particularly difficult for dogs, this can be a challenging hurdle for their owners. If you can't jump it with Beau, set it up where it would be difficult for him to go around it, and begin by calling him over it.

When you reach Step 4 and begin raising the third bar, adjust the first two bars so they always look like nice even steps, and make the width of the jump equal to each new height increment.

Progressing at Your Own Pace

It's reminder time again. Don't forget to use your jump command every time you send Beau, work every jump from both sides of him, and don't forget Step 5. In case you did, it's angled approaches and sending Beau to the jumps a little ahead of you.

For Safety's Sake

If Beau has a problem because this jump is so wide, keep it at its lowest and narrowest setting until after he learns the broad jump.

Spread Hurdle

Similar to the triple bar jump in appearance, the spread hurdle isn't quite as high and has two bars for little dogs, three bars for medium-size dogs and four bars for big dogs. Also, its bars are six inches apart, so it isn't as wide as the triple bar. Even so, the two obstacles are enough alike so that when Beau perfects either one he will probably learn the other easily. Make the introduction gradual if you're going from the spread to the triple, so he has time to learn that the new jump is higher and broader.

Bush Fence, Log Hurdles and Brush Jump

As pretty as its owners want to make it, the bush fence hurdle holds live plants, branches or decorative plastic plants, while the log hurdle is actually PVC pipes stacked in a pyramid. Both jumps are adjustable for dogs of different heights and both test Beau's ability to jump distance as well as height. Teach them after Beau knows the spread hurdle or the triple bar, and keep in mind that they are mighty different looking, so start low and go slow.

The brush jump is another hurdle Beau may find on a competitive course. It's similar to the bush fence hurdle, but the brush, or sometimes hay, is placed in the middle of a double bar jump.

Broad Jump, Long Jump or Long Hurdle

Remember the running broad jump you used to do on the playground? Well, now it's Beau's turn. The broad or long jump is made up of a number of boards (sections) or PVC pipes of slightly different heights, all low to the ground and spread out so the challenge is jumping distance rather than height. The distance required will be determined by Beau's height, so check the rule book(s) of the organization(s) you choose.

Sections of the broad jump are usually arranged in ascending order, so Beau will begin his jump at the lowest point and land after clearing the highest board, but sometimes they are arranged in an inverted V with the highest board in the middle. In agility jargon, this arrangement is called a hogback. Will Beau notice such low boards? You bet. The boards are painted for prime visibility, and a post at each end of the jump will also attract his attention.

Beau's broad jump will be brilliant if he jumps without hesitation in the required direction, clears every section without touching any of them, and sails across near the middle, between the corner posts. Walking on the jump or cutting corners is a no-no.

Stepping Off on the Right Paw

First, check the regulations to find out what length Beau will be required to jump and how many boards will make up his hurdle. Both will depend on his height and will vary among the organizations. Then spread your practice hurdle so it is half the regulation length. For medium and large dogs, you may have to temporarily remove a board when setting up your short practice hurdle because it's important to keep enough space between the boards so Beau isn't tempted to walk across instead of jumping. For tiny dogs, begin with one board when introducing this jump.

Teach the broad jump the same way you'd teach any other hurdle, using the five-step program, but watch out for two potential problems. Don't let Beau get in the habit of walking across the boards instead of jumping them or of cutting across the corner as he lands. The first time he makes either mistake, take action to keep it from happening again. Don't tell him he was wrong—agility training should always be positive—but skip the praise and set up a prop that makes it easier to do it right than wrong.

If Beau walked on the boards, it may be enough to turn one or more of the boards over on their sides. Did he still tiptoe through instead of jumping? Then it's time for the chicken wire remedy. Lay a piece of chicken wire either flat on the jump or shape it in a slight pyramid over the jump, making sure none of its sharp ends are turned upward. Walking on wire will quickly convince Beau that jumping is the way to go.

Cutting the corner before landing can be cured by laying a bar from one of the bar jumps down the length of the board jump. Place it close to the edge on the side Beau tends to cut, with its end extended a couple of feet. These props will make it tricky for you to jump the broad jump along with Beau, so skip that step. Make up for it by spending extra time on the run-bys.

A DOG'S EYE VIEW

Is Beau having more trouble learning an obstacle than you expected? Maybe it's because he sees it differently than you do. Before introducing any obstacle, get down to Beau's eye level (yes, even if he's a Chihuahua) and see what he sees when he looks ahead to the tunnel, ramp or hurdle. Do several obstacles look exactly the same? Does a mild obstacle look frightening? Knowing Beau well, and seeing the obstacle as he does, will help you tailor your training and handling to fit his needs.

Progressing at Your Own Pace

When everything is going well on the shortened broad jump, begin lengthening it gradually, eventually adding every board Beau will use in competition. Does that mean you can get rid of the chicken wire? No way. Continue using your props for at least a couple of months and don't hesitate to get them out again whenever the need arises. When working on angled approaches or angled exits, never make them so severe that Beau benefits by cutting the corner.

For Safety's Sake

If you use chicken wire, check it every so often. With continuous use, it could tear in a spot or two and you may have to turn sharp ends under more than once.

STOP FOR THE CLOCK

Imagine Beau barreling through an agility course, coming to an abrupt halt on command, sitting or lying down as directed, then resuming his run after the judge counts to five. That's what he will do on the pause table and in the pause box. Besides demonstrating control and trainability, learning this obstacle could save Beau's life. Imagine how much safer he will be on any outing when you can stop him in his tracks with one word.

Pause Table

The pause table is a sturdy, four-legged table with a nonslip surface (usually carpeting). It will never be higher than Beau's regulation jump height, but it may be lower.

Beau will perfect the pause table when he mounts it in one fluid motion on your command and/or signal and pauses on it for five seconds before dismounting (also on command) and heading for the next obstacle. Whether he pauses in the sit or the down position will depend on which organization's regulations are being used. Currently, USDAA requires the down position, UKC is handler's choice and AKC is judge's choice, with the judge informing the handlers before the start of the class.

Stepping Off on the Right Paw

If possible, begin with a table several inches lower than Beau's jump height and increase it gradually while teaching the sit and the down. Even though you want Beau to jump on the table, don't use your jump command or he may think it's a high broad jump and sail over it instead of landing on it. Instead, use "table" or another cue of your choice. With Beau on-lead, excite him, give your command and run to the table with him. Tap the table to inspire him to jump on it, and when he does, give hearty praise. Keep Beau on the table for several seconds with play or a treat, and practice until he leaps up with no hesitation.

When Beau relaxes on the table top, it's time to teach him to lie down on it, sit, or both, depending on which organization's agility trials you are preparing for. From then on, don't let him leave the table until he has performed one or the other. If Beau had obedience training, he already knows what "sit" and "down" mean. That will make training this obstacle much easier. If he doesn't down on command yet, give these methods a try.

Is Beau a chow hound? He'll learn what "sit" means if you hold a tempting treat in front of his nose, command "sit" and move the munchie over his head so his eyes follow it upward, his head tilts back and his rear meets the table. If Beau doesn't sit all the way down, use your free hand to push down and slightly forward on his rear. When it touches the table, give Beau the treat.

To teach your chow hound to lie down, tell him "down" as soon as he lands on the table, show him a goodie and lower it until your knuckles touch the table. As his head follows the treat, place the palm of your free hand on his shoulder blade and push sideways and down. Chances are, Beau will be so intent on the treat he'll be glad to devour it as he relaxes into the down. When Beau begins lying down for a treat without a push, be sure to wait until he's all the way down before giving the treat.

Duchess lies down on the pause table for a treat.

If treats don't entice Beau enough to make sits and downs come easily, try teaching the slide down. There are two methods. The first one works best with little dogs and the second with medium to large dogs. Both begin with your dog sitting. If Beau is a little guy, place your left hand on top of or just behind his withers (just back of where his neck meets his body) and your right hand, palm up, behind the top of his front legs near his elbows (never near his feet). Say "down," wait a second, then push down and slightly forward with your left hand while your right hand moves forward, sliding Beau's front legs out from under him. As soon as he's down, praise quietly while holding him in position for a few seconds. Then release him with cheery praise and a treat or toy.

Big Beau may slide down better if you reach over him with your left hand and grasp his left leg at elbow level while taking his right elbow in your right hand. Give the down command, wait a second, then lift both his legs up just enough so you can slide them forward into the down position. If Beau resists, lean on him with your chest while sliding his front legs. Praise softly while keeping him in the down position for a few seconds, then release and make a fuss over him.

Marilyn and Duchess demonstrate the slide down.

Little Beau will learn to sit if you put your right hand on his chest and cup his rear in your left hand. Say "sit," wait a second, then push back slightly with your right hand, slide it upward to stop under Beau's jawbone and tickle his chin. At the same time, push down and forward on Beau's rear with your left hand—just hard enough to make him sit. Hold him in place for a few seconds and release him with praise.

Big Beau will learn to sit if you hold the top of his collar in your right hand and place your left hand on his rear. Say "sit," wait a second, then push down and forward with your left hand while your right hand pulls the collar upward. Hold Beau in place for a few seconds, then release him and play.

Why did I tell you to "wait a second" between giving the "sit," or "down," command and guiding Beau into the correct position? Because he needs that second to show you when he knows what your words mean. One wonderful day he'll sit or down as soon as you say the words. "Way to go, Beau!"

The methods above work on confident, easily trainable dogs, but not every good agility dog fits into that category during novice training. Some dogs resist the down and a few fight it passionately. If Beau is one of them, he'll need more forceful training methods than should ever be taught on the agility course. Don't try to correct his attitude at home unless you are an experienced trainer. Attending a good obedience class somewhere other than where you do agility is the answer.

As soon as Beau sits and downs without physical guidance, begin teaching him signals as well as commands. You're allowed to use both simultaneously in competition, and at a noisy trial your dog will need all the help he can get. To signal the down, raise one arm up, palm out and elbow straight, then bring the arm down quickly. Say the command at the same time, so Beau makes the connection. To signal the sit, turn your palm up and raise your arm to waist or chest level with the elbow bent.

How will you know when Beau understands the signals? After a few weeks of practice (you can practice sits and downs at home without the pause table), try giving signals without the verbal cues. When Beau responds to

Jean reviews the "sit" signal with Annie.

signals alone, begin giving both the command and signal just as his front feet touch the table. That way he'll know immediately what position to settle in.

Beau has to learn to stay in position, on his own, for five seconds, but it's best to train him to stay for eight to ten seconds, and only occasionally release him on the five count. Up until now, you've been holding him in position for several seconds before releasing him. Now add the command "stay" and remove your hands but keep them only an inch or two from his body and be ready to stop him instantly if he tries to move before you release him. Tell Beau "okay" after ten seconds and release him with lots of praise, whether you had to help him stay in position or not. As he becomes steady on the table, gradually move away from him until you are at the end of the lead, but be prepared to come back and keep him in position if he tries to move before you release him.

Progressing at Your Own Pace

Once Beau jumps on the table happily, sits and downs on command and stays in place when you walk a few feet away, he's ready to try the table off-lead. A few feet from the obstacle, give your "table" command and send Beau out ahead of you. If he seems reluctant to leave you, a treat at the far end of the

Jean is "proofing" Annie by having a friend (me) act as judge. Before entering Annie in a trial, she needs to know if the dog will stay in position despite the distraction.

table may motivate him. Later, stop putting the treat on the table. Instead, wait until Beau jumps up on the obstacle, then go to him with the reward.

Gradually work on sending Beau to the table from longer distances and from either side of you, giving the sit or down command and signal just as Beau's toes touch the table. Now withhold the treat until Beau completes the stay and is released with a happy "okay."

When Beau is reliable on the table, ask an assistant to help you by standing nearby and doing the five-second countdown (to simulate a real agility trial). Be prepared to keep Beau in position if he becomes distracted. Occasionally use a table lower than Beau's regulation height because he may encounter lower ones in competition.

For Safety's Sake

While there is nothing dangerous about this obstacle, always check the practice table for steadiness before sending Beau. If it wobbles on uneven ground, it could hurt his confidence.

Pause Box

Used in advanced UKC and occasionally in USDAA agility, the pause box is usually made of PVC pipe and is approximately 48 inches square. In UKC agility it is raised between four and six inches off the ground, but in USDAA agility it may be flat on the ground and designated by four upright poles.

Beau will do fine on the pause box if he enters it from the most direct route, downs immediately on command (UKC permits a sit) with his head, body and legs inside the box, stays in position for the countdown and leaves on command, taking the most direct route to the next obstacle. Tails outside the box are not considered a fault.

Stepping Off on the Right Paw

Since Beau already knows the pause table, the transition to the box should be simple. First choose your cue. "Box" is used most often. Then put the box in a pleasant place (not in a puddle or ant hill), put Beau on-lead, give the command and walk him to the box. Command "down" (or "sit" if you prefer and are preparing for UKC events), and if Beau doesn't respond right away, help him the way you did when teaching the pause table. It won't be long before he makes the transition.

If Beau is a big boy, he might lie down with a leg or two hanging out of the box. Teach him to stay inside by gently pressing against his toes with your toes while telling him, "Tuck your toes." You may even say it in competition, although you aren't permitted to touch him.

Gradually take Beau through all the same steps you used when teaching the pause table, but before trying it off-lead, prepare him for all eventualities. Work him on different ground, indoors and out, such as grass, dirt and rubber matting, and if you are practicing for USDAA events use pause boxes made of PVC, wood, tape and just four upright posts.

TIRE, HOOP OR CIRCLE, WINDOW HURDLES AND WISHING WELL

More difficult than other hurdles because of the degree of accuracy they demand, the USDAA and AKC tire jumps consist of a tire or similar object hanging from a frame by four adjustable chains. USDAA's tire has a diameter between 17 and 20 inches, AKC's has a diameter of 24 inches, and UKC's hoop jump (not a tire) has a diameter of 29 inches.

AKC and UKC also have window hurdles. A wall suspended by a frame, usually with a square rather than circular opening, AKC's window is a 24-inch square or, if circular, has a diameter of 24 inches. UKC's window has an opening 14 inches wide and 30 inches high. All of these hurdles are adjustable and will be set at Beau's regulation jump height.

USDAA's Wishing Well, a circular base with a roof, has ample room beneath the roof for a dog to jump the base. A pole across the base will be set at Beau's regulation height. The tricky part is that the well might look like a panel jump to Beau, when it is really a spread hurdle.

Beau will handle the tire, hoop, window and wishing well hurdles by jumping through on your command without hesitation, in the indicated direction.

Teach these obstacles one at a time, following the same training steps for each one.

Stepping Off on the Right Paw

If your small dog had trouble learning an obstacle or two and you thought big dogs had the advantage in agility, these obstacles are payback time. Since only their height is adjustable, not their diameter, they are easier for small dogs and can be quite a squeeze for big bowsers.

The training Beau needs to do for this group of jumps is different from the steps used for the other hurdles. That's because in addition to jumping the hurdle, Beau has to place his body squarely through the center. This can be a challenge for high jumpers that are used to clearing obstacles with a foot to spare.

When introducing the tire, hoop or window jump, set them low enough so Beau can almost walk through but has to hop just a little. Now attach your loopless lead to Beau's collar and have him do a sit-stay about three feet from the opening and squarely in front of it. If he doesn't know the stay, ask a helper to hold him while you pass the end of his lead through the opening and go around to the other side.

Tap the inside bottom of the tire, hoop or window, make happy talk, show Beau a treat through the opening—whatever it takes to get him excited—then call him, using a new command, not your regular jump command. "Tire," "Hoop," and "Window," are obvious commands, but anything unique to each of these obstacles will do. Use your lead to make sure Beau trots through the obstacle and doesn't try to go around it or come through the space between the tire and the frame. Then praise him, no matter how much help he needed, and try again.

When Beau understands the obstacle, put your loopless tab on him and try run-bys. Start several feet from the jump and directly in line with it. Try to get Beau to focus on the obstacle, aim him well and hold the tab until he begins his jump. Then meet him on the other side for a victory dance. Practice a couple more times, then change hands on the tab so Beau learns to enter the obstacle from either side of you. So far, so good? Now try it off-lead with you on either side of Beau.

When Beau has mastered the first height, it's time to move the tire up two inches. From then on continue as before, starting with the on-lead recall and progressing to run-bys with the tab and, finally, off-lead work on either side. Stay at each two-inch increment at least a week, and once you reach regulation height, practice at that height from then on so Beau becomes accustomed to using the amount of effort that it takes him to get through the obstacle without a bump.

What if Beau tries to go under the tire when you raise it? Remember chicken wire? Attach it between the tire and the frame (get rid of sharp edges) and leave it there for several training sessions. Plexiglas also works.

When introducing the wishing well, walk Beau around it several times so he knows it isn't just another panel jump. Then set the pole low at the far end of the jump, or put two single bar jumps across the well in ascending height (keep them both low). The object is to help Beau see that this is a spread jump.

Making the tire jump fun for Duchess.

Train this jump as you did the tire, hoop or window and move the pole back to the center, or remove the double bar training aid, when Beau obviously understands the obstacle. Then gradually bring the center pole up to Beau's competitive jump height.

Progressing at Your Own Pace

After Beau performs these obstacles off-lead, at full height, from either side of you, gradually begin sending him ahead of you to the hurdle. Also, do some long recalls through it. When approaching an obstacle from a straight line becomes easy for Beau, begin working on angled approaches.

For Safety's Sake

Some day at a practice session you may be tempted to use the tire (or window) jump as is, instead of bothering to raise it to Beau's jump height. After all, how can jumping a little lower hurt anything? Well, once Beau is good at this obstacle he will do it the same way every time and probably won't notice or react quickly enough to a slightly lower hurdle. If he does everything right and bangs his head anyway, he'll no longer trust the obstacle.

When doing run-bys with Beau on the tab, keep one eye on the jump so you don't ram into it in your eagerness to line Beau up correctly before letting go.

WATER HURDLE

The UKC water hurdle is two low ramps with platforms across a shallow pool. The length of the gap between the platforms, which Beau will jump, depends on his size, with 30 inches being maximum. The platforms are large and safe and the ramps are around a foot long.

Beau will whiz over the water hurdle if he mounts the ramp in the right direction without hesitation, leaps over the water from one platform to the other and exits down the opposite ramp.

Stepping Off on the Right Paw

This jump is shorter than the long hurdle and the ramps are low, so teach Beau the long hurdle and any obstacle with ramps first, and the transition to the water hurdle will be easy.

Shorten the gap between the platforms to half of what Beau will eventually jump, and with him on-lead, walk him up the ramp to the platform. Then step around to the other side and use your voice to excite Beau while tapping the opposite platform. When Beau focuses on it, tell him to jump and back up a little. As soon as he lands, guide him down the ramp and give him lots of praise.

When Beau understands the obstacle, try it off-lead. If all goes well, do run-bys by approaching it from several feet away with you on either side of Beau. Then gradually lengthen the gap between the platforms about two inches a week, going through all the introductory steps with each increase.

Progressing at Your Own Pace

When Beau does the water hurdle at regulation distance off-lead, begin adding angled approaches with him on either side of you, sometimes sending him to the obstacle ahead of you.

For Safety's Sake

Though its name makes it sound tricky, this isn't a dangerous obstacle for Beau. You, on the other hand, should either keep one eye on where you are going or wear a swim suit.

PLATFORM JUMP

The platform jump is composed of two low platforms with a low hurdle between them.

Despite its name, this UKC obstacle really isn't a jump at all. Instead, it's a test of control and trainability. Beau will give a fine performance on the platform jump if he steps up on the platform in the direction indicated, sits all the way down immediately, gets up and cleanly hops the hurdle, then sits all the way down on the second platform before exiting the obstacle. He may enter and exit the platforms from any side, except the side closest to the hurdle.

Stepping Off on the Right Paw

Start with the platforms a little closer and the hurdle a little lower than it will be in competition. With Beau beside you wearing his loopless lead, give the obstacle a name and go over it right beside him. If he has already learned to sit on command during pause table training, teaching this obstacle will be much easier. If not, use the methods in the pause table section to teach Beau how to sit on this obstacle.

At first, praise Beau when he sits, when he hops the hurdle and again when he sits on the other side, but gradually withhold praise until he completes all three parts and exits successfully. Never let Beau hop the hurdle or exit the second platform until after he sits all the way down. Gradually work up to run-bys and finally off-lead work on either side of him.

When you increase the hurdle height and the distance between the platforms, go back on-lead and walk through it with Beau the first few times (if you can), or simply do run-bys on-lead. Gradually work your way back to off-lead work on either side, but don't rush. If Beau thinks you're in a hurry, he may start missing his sits and you'll have to start back at the beginning.

Progressing at Your Own Pace

Gradually add angled entrances and try sending Beau to the obstacle a little ahead of you. Although you are allowed to tell Beau to "sit," "jump," "sit," the top dogs do it all automatically.

For Safety's Sake

Warm Beau up well before practicing this obstacle. Even though the hop over the hurdle is low, he has to do it from a stop, without the momentum of running or trotting up to the jump.

CHAPTER 4

GETTING *Started*

Is Beau more like a Basset Hound or a Border Collie? Is he little and quick, big and clumsy, or somewhere in between? Is he outgoing or timid? Laid-back or a live wire? Purebred or an all-American mutt?

ASSESSING YOUR DOG'S AGILITY APTITUDE

As long as Beau is healthy and fit, he can succeed in agility no matter what his body type. In fact, training for an agility career helps clumsy dogs become as graceful as their structure allows them to be. It also helps retiring dogs gain confidence and gives over-active dogs a positive outlet for their excess energy. Of course, some dogs are born with more aptitude for agility than other dogs, and all dogs need some advance preparation to thoroughly enjoy agility class. Let's see where Beau fits. Answering these questions, and reading the explanations that follow, will help you assess his aptitude and prepare him for his agility adventure.

Activity Levels and Desire for Attention

Don't look, just guess. What's Beau doing right now? Is he pouncing on a toy, chasing after the kids, napping on the throw rug, looking longingly at his doggie dish, or poking his head up under this book to elicit your attention?

Would Beau rather play catch than eat? Is going for a walk the high point of his day? Does being petted make him wiggle in ecstasy, or would he rather be left alone?

For attention-seeking dogs with high activity levels, agility training is like a hot fudge sundae to a chocoholic. Immediate gratification. The combination of creative exercise and your undivided attention will make agility class the best hour in Beau's week. Not only that, but with purpose in his life (a.k.a. a real job), and the training to go with it, he'll soon become an even brighter and better behaved companion.

Most successful agility dogs have average activity levels at home even though they exude excitement when running the course. If Beau enjoys attention, turns on for a treat or loves games with balls or toys, he'll be easy to motivate and should succeed at this sport.

If sleeping is Beau's favorite pastime and a quick pat from you will do, perhaps he isn't a good candidate for agility. But if you want to try, he may rally and try too. Just don't put 10 weeks of agility classes on your credit card until you test him out. Fill your pocket with his favorite treats and take him somewhere other than home (he's in a rut at home) for the test. A friend's fenced yard will do. Take along a four-foot or so length of PVC pipe or a broomstick, and two cans or boxes. The cans or boxes should be tall enough to make a hurdle just lower than the height of Beau's elbow when you put your stick across them.

Now get silly. Run across that little hurdle, clapping for Beau to join you. If he doesn't, try it again. When he does, get more excited over him than you've ever been before and tell him how great he is as you give him a treat. Then try it again. Tap the jump and invite him over. Is his tail wagging yet? Throw the treat across the hurdle and race him for it. If you win, give it to him anyway. Make a fuss. Do his shining eyes say he just had a wake-up call? Agility could be just what he needs to make his life interesting and lengthen it, too. But first, he may have to lose some weight and gain some condition. If Beau slept away most of the last couple years, tell your veterinarian you want to start agility and follow his or her recommendations for conditioning.

What if Beau watched you jump, watched you jump again, then turned his back and walked away from the silly scene? Sometimes timing is everything, so don't give up yet. Try again another day, and make sure it's before, not after, his dinner. If he still isn't interested, he probably never will be.

Temperament and Sociability

When your friends visit, does Beau beg for their attention, hide behind the sofa, defend his home by growling at them, or behave the same as when he's alone with you?

When Beau sees a strange dog on neutral territory (not near either dog's home), does he want to play with it, ignore it or pick a fight?

Have you ever walked Beau in a noisy, crowded place? If not, try it near a mall or supermarket entrance. Does Beau prance happily in hopes of being noticed, tuck his tail and stick close to your legs, put up his hackles, or act as if nothing is new?

What scares Beau? Is he terrified of thunder, any sudden loud noises, strange dogs or new people? When startled, does he recover quickly? If you don't know, drop a large book or pan about 10 feet from him when he's in the kitchen (or any room without a carpet) and isn't looking in your direction. It will startle most dogs (and most people), and that's fine. What you want to know is how long it takes him to recover. Is he fine in a few seconds, or is he still waiting wide-eyed for the sky to fall?

No matter how sociable Beau is, he may surprise you at an agility event. Doggie amusement parks are like human amusement parks: They exude a festive aura of excitement and are often crowded. An appreciative audience adds to the fun as well as to the noise level. Sometimes you (and Beau) will even sense an undertone of stress, as seasoned handlers become caught up in the competition and novices fret over their first try.

Beau will handle the bustling place best if he takes new things in stride. It's ideal if he obviously enjoys the novelty without becoming overly excited.

Maybe Beau is so outgoing he'll bounce with glee and want to make friends with the new people and meet all the other dogs. If so, convincing him to focus on the course may be a challenge at first, but he'll probably settle down after a few events. Help him by practicing in new places (you don't have to go far—even your neighbor's yard is a new place to him). Many top agility dogs were over-enthusiastic at the start of their careers. While their eagerness was a hindrance at first, it was an advantage in the long run, as it kept them competing at their peak for several years.

If Beau is insecure around new people, places or dogs, he'll find an agility event frightening instead of fun, unless he's been prepared in advance. Classes will help, but what he needs most is socialization. Later in this chapter, I'll tell you all about it. Please give it a try. Even if you decide not to do agility, socialization will make Beau a happier dog and a better companion. Can insecure dogs ever learn to like agility? You bet. But by then, socialization has helped them overcome their fears.

A dog that is either so defensive or so scared that he growls at your friends is not a good candidate for agility training. Neither is a dog that picks fights with other dogs. That doesn't mean brawling Beau will never be able to do agility, but he'll have to successfully graduate from a good obedience course first. At obedience school you will receive professional help in training Beau, and he will gain confidence and manners as he masters the skills that will make him a more reliable friend. Best of all, it won't even set you back in starting agility. Most dogs benefit from having some obedience training first, but for some dogs it's an absolute necessity.

Beau may love the world and everyone in it but still be so noise sensitive that the cacophony near the agility course makes him jumpy and keeps him from concentrating. For many dogs, there's an easy solution. All you need is a tape recording of a major trial—one held at a dog show with spectators clapping, dogs barking and an occasional announcement over the loudspeaker. If noise bothers Beau, attend your first trial without him just to watch (it's a good idea anyway), and take a tape recorder along. Record an hour or so of the competition and bring Beau the soundtrack. Play it the first time while Beau does something he loves, like eating dinner, and don't turn it up all the way. Turn it on when you and Beau are playing and use it as music to pet by. Gradually play it as loud as it sounded the day you recorded it, but no louder. Soon Beau will be so used to the noise he won't react at all. Thunderous applause at an event may still spook him a little, because hearing it in a strange place is still different from hearing it in his own living room. But it won't be half as scary as it would be if he never heard it before.

Training and Retention

Does Beau come every time you call him, or only when he wants to? Does he sit or down on command, and will he stay in place several seconds until you tell him it's okay to get back up? When you take him for a walk, do strangers ask, "Who's walking who?" or does he stay close to you without pulling?

Does Beau do any tricks like shaking hands, barking on command, catching a ball or retrieving a stick? Is he eager to show off or does he respond reluctantly most of the time?

Where does Beau live? Is he a house dog, a yard dog or half and half?

The more a dog learns, the more he is able to learn. When a dog is taught new things often, learning becomes a habit. Also, most of the commands or tricks we teach our dogs build on each other. For example, a dog has to know how to sit on command before he can learn to shake hands or do a sit-stay.

If Beau already had obedience training (I prefer to call it companion dog training, because it teaches owners and dogs how to please each other and become better friends), he is way ahead in the agility game. All agility dogs must respond to a few commands. But even if you didn't train Beau to obey any commands, he still has a head start if you taught him some tricks. If he hams up his handshake, or drops a ball in your lap when he wants to play catch or fetch, he's learned how to learn and that's a big plus in agility training.

If Beau is stubborn or hesitant about performing tricks or obeying commands he already learned, it might be your fault. Perhaps you played the role of drill sergeant and he couldn't wait to ship out of boot camp. Or maybe you went too fast, and he's still unsure of his responses. Did you praise him every step of the way? If you can look back on your training sessions and be positive you gave Beau plenty of time and ample encouragement, and he still hated every minute of it, test him before committing to an agility class. The test described in the section "Activity Levels and Desire for Attention" will work just fine.

Does it matter if Beau is a house dog or lives outside? Yes. House dogs and their owners are roommates. Sharing the same living quarters, they get to know each other well enough to read each other's body language. That kind of closeness makes them better partners in a quick-response sport like agility. Will Beau be an agility dropout if he's a kennel dog or yard dog? Not if you give him sufficient quality time. Agility is both the cake and the icing to outdoor dogs, as it gives them what they want most: their owner's undivided attention. And boy, are they willing to work for it! But if two dogs and two handlers of similar ability were competing on an advanced agility course, and one was an outside dog and the other a roomie, I'd bet the roomie would win.

Readiness

Does Beau travel well? Will he relax in a dog crate?

Attending agility events, or even classes, requires taking Beau along in your vehicle. If he's a good traveler, he'll arrive ready to run, climb and jump. But if riding makes him nervous or carsick, performing his best may be out of the question.

The safest way for Beau to travel is securely crated in a bed created especially for dogs. Even if you prefer having him on the seat beside you, you'll need a crate so he has a familiar place to rest at agility trials. When Beau learns to relax in his crate, he'll have a cozy part of home with him wherever he goes and will get the rest he needs to do his best. I know some of you are thinking, "No way, not my dog," but people who love their dogs every bit as much as you love yours swear by crates. Please learn more about them before rejecting the idea. For help in turning Beau into a good traveler and an introduction to crates, see "Keeping Beau Safe and Comfortable on the Road," in Chapter 5.

Grace, Body Awareness and Hardiness

Are Beau's legs and body in proportion like a Labrador Retriever's, or does he have stubby legs like a Basset Hound or long, lean legs like a Greyhound? Is he quick and nimble, slow and steady, awkward and clumsy or stiff and hesitant? When there is a low obstacle such as a log in his path, does he jump it in glee, scramble over it awkwardly or go around it? What does he think of rain? Does he ignore it, play in every puddle, or tip-toe around puddles as if he thought alligators lurked under the surface?

Where's Bandit?

He's proving that smart dogs with high activity levels don't need long legs to succeed at this sport.

Just as we weren't all born equal when it comes to gymnastic potential, our dogs don't have equal agility potential. Their body structure mirrors the jobs they traditionally performed. For example, Basset Hounds are low to the ground because that's the best place to be when trailing rabbits by scent, while Greyhounds are the lanky track stars of the dog world.

What's the ideal body for an agility dog? One that's in proportion—in other words, average looking. Dogs with especially short legs may not be able to run a course as fast as their leggier competitors. But many dogs with short legs and big hearts earn agility titles, because agility is about control and accuracy as well as speed. In fact, it's not unusual for a Dachshund to be the darling of the audience. Even if "slow and steady" describes Beau, he'll still get good scores if you concentrate on precision and accuracy.

What about those stilt-legged sighthounds? Like many tall dogs, some of them need help with rear body awareness when learning the contact obstacles, and tunnel training may go slowly. Finished performances are another story. Few dogs of any other body structure can dart around an agility course with the grace and speed of a motivated sighthound.

What if bumbling Beau trips over his own toes and your friends nicknamed him Thunderfoot? Agility training, especially rear body awareness exercises (see "Introducing Obstacles in Order" later in this chapter) will improve his moves. Elevate the contact obstacles very slowly so he doesn't take a spill, and make sure he can handle each hurdle height easily before raising the jumps. By the time he's ready to perform a whole course, he may be slow but he'll be a lot more sure-footed.

Do you ever have to help your Beau do something he used to do easily, like jump in the car—and now that you think about it, has it been a long time since he jumped or climbed anything? Check with your veterinarian before signing up for an agility class. If he or she thinks agility work would be beneficial, take it slow and easy and always do at least 10 minutes of warm-up exercises with your dog before heading for the obstacles (see "Conditioning Your Team" later in this chapter). If your veterinarian advises against agility, take the advice. Arthritic joints and agility obstacles aren't a good match.

If Beau is a water baby, count it as an agility blessing. Dogs that think getting wet is an added attraction have an advantage at outdoor events. Some dogs don't seem to care one way or the other, and that's also good. But if Beau puts his tail between his legs and pouts when he has to potty in the morning dew, it's going to take time to prepare him for wet agility courses.

Attending only indoor events is also an option, but it limits your agility opportunities.

Now that you know more about how Beau's activity level, disposition, previous training and natural grace affect his agility aptitude, let's concentrate on the other half of your agility team—you.

ASSESSING YOUR AGILITY APTITUDE

Agility is good for people. It can alleviate stress by focusing on fun, and enhance your social life by introducing you to the lively world of "dog people." It can help you stay fit while strengthening the bond between you and Beau. It can even give you an excuse to travel, as agility trials are held somewhere in the United States nearly every weekend.

Agility can be an inexpensive pastime or an expensive and consuming avocation. It all depends on your level of intensity—how much time you are willing to spend training your dog and yourself, and how much money you can devote to entry fees and travel. Some people participate just for the pure enjoyment of training their dog and do most of their agility in their own yard. Others want to earn agility titles and still others aren't satisfied unless they win blue ribbons. Which type are you? How far do you want to go? Does your dog match your aspirations?

You and Beau can have fun with agility by placing homemade obstacles in the backyard and playing on them without ever attending a class. Or you can work toward winning a national championship and maybe even securing a spot on the USA team at the World Agility Championships. Chances are, you'll opt for something in between. The important thing is to set realistic but challenging goals and work toward them, one small, satisfying step at a time.

For you and Beau to enjoy your agility journey, your goals should take his body type and temperament into consideration. For example, if Beau isn't built for speed, he'll never win agility's Grand Prix but he's perfectly capable of earning titles. Ready to get started? The next section will help you prepare Beau mentally for the fun and challenges of his new sport.

SOCIALIZATION

Beau will enjoy agility more and perform better if he is well socialized. If he is still a young puppy, you have an ideal situation. Take advantage of it. You can only raise Beau once, so give him the gift of early socialization.

Take every opportunity to socialize your dog. Marilyn hands her friend a treat to give to Duchess.

Dogs remember all their lives what they learn about the world when they are between seven and 16 weeks of age. Those nine short weeks affect their personality, making them brave or bashful, fun-loving or fearful, eager to try new tricks or resentful of training. This short period of high retention is a throwback to the dog's wild ancestors and corresponds to when wild pups or cubs ventured out of the den for the first time. From that moment on, they learned lessons in survival. Everything had to be ingrained in a hurry, because when young animals make a mistake in the wild they rarely get a second chance.

Even though Beau's ancestors have been domesticated for centuries, puppies are still programmed to learn how to handle their environment during their first four months of life. With or without your help, Beau will gain insights into what's safe and what's dangerous. Is he under four months old? Lucky you. You have an opportunity to introduce him to a friendly world and help him grow up trusting and confident—a prime candidate for agility training.

Chances are your Beau is well over four months old. Did you raise him from a puppy? If you enjoyed his puppy antics and showed him off to your friends, I bet you did just fine and he is well-adjusted and secure. But maybe you got him as an adult and don't know if he had a pleasant or poor puppy-hood. Then again, maybe you do know. You know because he cringes when your friends try to pet him, or hides behind your legs when you visit new places, or cowers when you are dressing and take your belt out of the closet. Will he succeed as an agility dog even though he was ignored—or worse—as a puppy? Maybe. Plenty of abused puppies have overcome their past and went on to triumph at a variety of dog events, including agility. The first step in reconditioning Beau is to stop blaming everything he does on his pitiful puppyhood. It's over. Beau may have gotten off to a bad start, but he's got you now and that makes him a lucky dog. Turn off the pity and you'll start making progress. When should you start? Yesterday. But today will do just fine.

A Game with Two Rules

Socializing Beau isn't a step-by-step process, like agility training. It's easier than that because it's all part of daily life. Every time Beau visits a new place (even if it's just on the next block), does something he has never done (even if it's just playing with a new toy) or meets a new person, he is being social-ized. Socializing Beau will be a lot like playing games with him, and, like all games, it has rules. Rule one is never pet or even talk to Beau when he is acting fearful. Rule two is always praise Beau for behaving bravely.

Is Beau retiring around strangers and leery of new places or objects? If he is, remember the first rule of socialization when you have friends over or take him on an outing. When Beau backs up or cringes with his tail between his legs, don't reassure him by cajoling or petting, as he will interpret your ac-tions as praise. Anything he is praised for he'll want to repeat again and again, so hiding behind your legs or tucking his tail could become his learned response to anything new. On the other hand, never yank him toward the feared person or object. Treatment like that turns a slight scare into total terror.

What should you do when Beau is afraid of something? Just approach the new object yourself, caress it as if it was a long lost love and, using your happiest voice, invite Beau over to see the wonderful thing. Sitting down by the feared object may entice Beau to join you. Still scared, but curious too, Beau may make his way over on his belly and examine the object of his fears with his nose outstretched. After he approaches and examines the object, praise him for being a brave boy. If the object isn't breakable or too big, roll it away from (never toward) Beau. It may arouse his natural chasing instinct and make him pounce on the object in play.

Don't be discouraged if Beau fears something as silly as a new recliner in the living room or even a fireplug. Before he is socialized, Beau may see the bogeyman everywhere. Fears fade slowly, and Beau needs to be put in socializing situations as often as possible. Here's a few quick and easy shortcuts.

Help at Home

Get Beau used to loud noises by making noise every time something good is about to happen to him. Put his dinner in a metal pan and stir it with a metal spoon. Sometimes be clumsy and drop the pan (no closer than a few feet from him) before you fill it. Does Beau eagerly await the children coming home from school? Then announce their arrival with applause and cheers. Give Beau his own noisemaker too. An empty plastic half gallon or gallon milk jug works great. Just lay it on the floor and ignore it. It might be a while before Beau approaches it, but eventually he may become brave enough to drag the jug, then shake it, and finally bang it against table legs and walls. What will Beau learn from all this? He'll learn that noise isn't so scary because sometimes it brings good things and other times he can create and control it.

Take along treats when taking Beau for a walk. If someone stops to talk, ask them to give him a treat. The more people Beau meets and the more sights and sounds he gets used to, the better prepared he'll be for agility. As his fears diminish, his trainability will expand. But even more important, once Beau buries his bogeymen, he'll be a happier dog.

START SMART

While mentally preparing Beau for agility, prepare yourself as well. Before signing up for classes, attend an agility trial or two without Beau, just to watch. Unless the event is held in an arena complete with bleachers, chairs may not be provided, so take a comfortable lawn chair along and set it up at ringside. Not only will watching help you decide if this is the sport for you, but it will help you learn to visualize an ideal performance. At first every attempt may look terrific, but after concentrating for a couple of hours you'll be able to recognize smooth performances and superb handling. Study the best handlers and the top dogs and you will soon have a mental picture of what you want to achieve. Never stop observing. No matter how competitive you and Beau become, you can always learn something new just by watching at ringside.

Agility judges use hand signals and a whistle to indicate faults. At UKC trials they also call out "Fault" on major errors so the handler has an opportunity to try the obstacle again. The number of points assessed for each mistake varies with the organization. Judges don't use too many different signals, so after watching for a few minutes you'll have seen most of them. If you don't know what they mean, ask someone who had a dog in competition.

You may hear the judge blow a whistle indicating that a dog is excused or eliminated from competition. That happens when a dog makes a big mistake, like leaving the course entirely or fouling the course (agility jargon for going potty).

Besides watching the top handlers in the advanced classes, be sure to see some novice dogs run as well. You'll soon realize that the judges have seen it all and nothing you and Beau might do as beginners will shock them. Agility is such a young sport that most of today's top handlers and judges were beginners like you just a decade or so ago. Most of them still remember how it felt when butterflies fluttered wildly in their bellies.

Read the Rules of the Game

All competitive sports have rules and good players know them well. As soon as you decide which style(s) of agility to train for, contact the organization(s) and request a rule book (see Chapter 2 or the Appendix for the addresses of agility organizations). Even though your agility instructor (if you have one) will prepare you for competition, knowing the rules, and how your organization will score your performance, is your responsibility.

OFF TO AGILITY SCHOOL

You probably won't want to landscape your yard with agility obstacles (at least not at first), so you'll need a place where you and Beau can learn and practice. Even if you have a spare quarter acre and own your own obstacles, it's still best to attend classes if they are available in your area. You and Beau could adopt bad habits by training alone, and starting out right is always easier than retraining later. Besides, agility classes are fun. They're full of dynamic people who enjoy activities with their dogs.

Depending on where you live, you may have two options: joining an agility club or taking lessons from a private instructor. To find out if there is an agility club in your area, contact the AKC, the UKC, the USDAA and the NADAC. Their addresses are in the Appendix. Tell them where you live and they will help you find the agility club closest to you.

Private teachers specializing in agility classes may be located through ads in the telephone book, the classifieds, pet supply stores and veterinarians' offices.

If both club and privately owned classes are available, which one should you choose? The one with the right instructor for you and Beau—one whose methods and attitude match your goals and personality. Here's help.

Choosing an Instructor

When choosing an agility school, observe a session or two of each beginner class available in your area. All good agility instructors have several things in common, so look for the following attributes:

- Good agility instructors are concerned with safety. Before signing up for lessons, look at the equipment. The obstacles should be sturdy and stable, with no rough edges and not a hint of a wobble. The courses should have good footing—sufficient traction and no hidden surprises such as sharp rocks or protruding roots. Although several dogs may be negotiating different obstacles at the same time, safe classes will still appear organized, not chaotic, and will emphasize accuracy above speed.

- Good agility instructors are masters of motivation. They communicate clearly and are upbeat, with a friendly, helpful attitude. When necessary, they will explain the same technique in several different ways until their student understands. Anyone can give directions, but only the best teachers can provide answers to any training situation and are willing to spend time solving individual problems.

- Good agility instructors teach their students to use praise, toys and treats, never force, to motivate their dogs.

- Good agility instructors have a lesson plan—one that matches the goals set by their students.

- Good agility instructors have a high success rate. Their schools produce titled dogs of a variety of breeds, including those breeds not built to be top agility contenders. Also, their advanced students place high in competition.

- Good agility instructors are flexible. They can adapt their methods to fit the changing needs of their students.

- Good agility instructors take time with all of their students, not just the ones with potentially winning dogs. They are not prejudiced against any breed and can work within different handler and dog shapes, sizes, ages and other limitations.

- Good agility instructors know that only perfect practice builds perfect performances. They go slow, keep the obstacles low, and make sure every dog and handler in the class has a firm foundation.

- Good agility instructors constantly challenge their students.

- Good agility instructors have a trained eye. They can evaluate a dog and handler's strengths and weaknesses, and make suggestions to improve performance.

- Good agility instructors respect their students and are respected by their students. Look for empathy—an awareness that everyone in the class has feelings, including the dogs.

Preparing for Class: What You Should Know Before You Go

Agility is exercise and no one exercises well on a full stomach, so don't feed Beau before class. Working him on a empty tummy won't do him any harm and will probably make him more alert and eager to earn treats.

Check Beau's toenails before attending class. If they make clicking sounds when he walks on a hard floor, they are too long and will interfere, or even hurt, when he tries to negotiate obstacles. He should also be free of fleas. No dog can learn when he has to stop and scratch.

Just before leaving for class, give Beau sufficient time to relieve himself in your fenced yard, or take him for a walk. Going potty on the agility course is a real no-no. The class has to stop until it's cleaned up and the remaining scent is distracting to the other dogs. However, accidents do happen. Even though you give Beau every opportunity to relieve himself before class, he may still soil the course someday, so carry a roll of paper towels just in case. Taking action is always better than just standing there looking embarrassed.

Beau is going to love agility class, so if getting him used to his crate or making him feel comfortable in the car are potential problems, the drive to class (in addition to crate training at home) should help solve them. Put the crate in your vehicle and secure it well so it won't slide around or (horrors!) roll over. Then cushion the floor of the crate with a soft pad (a carpet sample or old pillow are fine) and tell Beau to "kennel up." You may have to help him (read: push him in) at first, but whether he enters on his own or at your insistence, reward him with a nice chew toy as soon as he is inside. Eventually he may relate riding in the crate to the fun of attending agility classes. Then he will be happy to climb in on his own. For additional help in making Beau a good traveler, see "Keeping Beau Safe and Comfortable on the Road" in Chapter 5.

When you collect Beau's class equipment (buckle collar, loopless lead, toys and treats), check your own attire, too. Are you wearing comfortable shoes with good traction and support? Good. Now double tie the laces so they won't open and trip you. If you have long hair, secure it back out of your face so it doesn't block your vision, and exchange dangling earrings for button types. Remove anything that moves enough to distract your dog or get caught on an obstacle, such as a necktie, sash-style belt or bangle bracelet. Your clothing should be mentally comfortable, too. Agility is too much fun to worry about grass stains.

What to Expect

When you arrive for your first class, Beau's attitude may range from excitement at seeing so many dogs and people, to fear of the mild commotion. No two agility schools are the same because instructors all have different personalities. In fact, even within the same school each new group of students lends its own tone to the class.

Prices vary between schools, but are usually competitive within an area. To give you some idea of what to expect, I interviewed agility judge John Loomis and his wife Patricia, owners of Alibi Kennel and Training Facility in Jacksonville, Arkansas. Alibi's novice agility class costs $89. It runs for eight weeks, with one lesson per week. Classes are limited to 10 students and there is about an hour of actual dog work. Besides introducing the obstacles and simple sequences, the Loomises spend a lot of time working on the "stay" or "wait" commands. They also rest the dogs and handlers frequently and use the breaks to discuss rules and strategy. "We always keep the challenge just a little beyond what the students can do easily, so they don't get over-confident or bored," Pat says.

Students are welcome to practice on Alibi's equipment on Saturdays, providing the Loomises are home. They are also expected to practice at home—15 minutes, two or three times a week, is recommended. The Loomises suggest they make a few simple jumps out of PVC pipe, stick PVC in the ground for weave poles and get a couple of concrete blocks and a sturdy 10-foot-long board to simulate the dog walk. "With four or five jumps, weave poles and the makeshift dog walk, students can do enough agility to learn a lot at home and only have to come to class once a week to work on the bigger equipment," Pat explains. At the end of eight weeks, most dogs do all the novice obstacles and are able to run a simple course off-lead at a lower height than they will run in competition.

Once the Loomises know a student well, the student is invited to practice on Alibi's equipment (with a partner for safety) any time there is no class in session.

With a weekly class, practice at home and occasional practice on Alibi's equipment, how long does it take until a beginner is ready to enter a real trial? The typical novice takes at least six to eight months to prepare for competition, say the Loomises, but there are exceptions. Dogs that already had obedience training sometimes get by in three to four months, not counting weave poles. Weaving up to Alibi's standards takes at least a year of practice (AKC and UKC do not include weave poles on novice courses).

Although obedience training gives most dogs a head start, sometimes previous experience in competitive obedience is a mixed blessing, because obedience is always performed with the dog on the handler's left side. "One of the most difficult things an obedience handler has to learn is working the dog off both sides of the body," Pat Loomis says. "It's difficult for the dog, too, especially when it is used to formal obedience."

"Another difficult thing for obedience buffs is breaking the habit of the dog watching the handler's every move instead of looking toward the next obstacle," Pat adds. "If a dog is food-trained, we have a hard time breaking it from watching its handler's hand. Most novice handlers unintentionally add to the problem by waving their hand around. Meanwhile, their dog goes everywhere the hand goes and doesn't focus on the obstacles ahead."

Is there a remedy? "Sure," says Pat. "We have them put their hands in their pockets. To motivate their dog, they can toss a treat over the hurdle in front of the dog or place a treat on the ground just past the exit of a contact obstacle. It isn't long before the dog watches where it's going."

CREATING YOUR OWN AGILITY CLASSES

Agility has become so popular that there aren't enough established agility clubs and schools to fill the demand in some parts of the country. Many groups successfully solved that problem by building or buying equipment and creating their own classes. Some of these new groups have instructors with agility experience, but others are made up entirely of novices helping each other. Does it work? Sure—as long as the training methods are sound.

Compared to established dog sports such as obedience and field trials, agility is in its infancy and some of its greatest gurus were novices only a decade ago. "Those of us who started agility in the beginning had no mentors," says agility instructor and judge Mike Bond of Naperville, Illinois. "We were it. Most of us learned and evolved as we went. Now newer groups have the advantage of drawing from this collective experience."

One new club recently asked Bond to observe their agility classes and make recommendations. "What I observed," he says, "was an agility three-ring circus. Equipment was all set up at full height. Dogs of all sizes and abilities were running full bore in every direction. I saw one handler trip over a tug-toy thrown by another handler. A Schipperke ran into one end of an open tunnel, only to turn round midway and race out with a Lab that had entered from the opposite end in hot pursuit. One handler spent several minutes meticulously setting jump bars for her Maltese, only to have them

Creating your own class just takes some equipment and a few enthusiastic people who want to help each other learn the sport. Jean's dog demonstrates the form that already earned him a leg without the benefit of formal classes.

reset by a man working his Doberman before she got to the end of the row to start her dog. On the far side of the ring, two handlers rushed their dogs up opposite ends of the dog walk. When they realized what had happened, one woman grabbed her Golden Retriever and lifted him off. But the owner of the Rottweiler going in the opposite direction didn't react as quickly. She watched in horror as her dog launched himself off the middle of the obstacle to avoid a collision. This was not a class for the faint-hearted."

Bond gave the club members the guidelines that follow to help them organize productive and safe classes. His suggestions will work for any group that wants to get together and learn agility, so don't let lack of a local instructor stop you from enjoying this sport. Get a few people together and start your own class.

A foundation in practical obedience is a prerequisite to attending Bond's own classes, as dogs must be under control when learning agility (see "Obedience for Agility Dogs" in this chapter). They should come when called, on- and off-lead, and obey commands such as sit, down and stand. Even if a dog learned obedience at home, Bond believes it should be exposed to some type of class situation (such as Kindergarten Puppy Training) to become comfortable enough to concentrate amid the commotion of other dogs and handlers. If your group offers obedience courses in addition to agility, they should be held at a different location than your agility class. Dogs soon realize they are expected to behave at obedience school, but do their best agility work when they think it's all for fun.

Instead of overpowering novice dogs with all the obstacles at once, Bond divides his beginners class into six categories: flatwork, jumping, tunnels, contact obstacles, weave poles and handling strategy.

Flatwork means working the dogs on the ground (between obstacles) and involves close and distance work. Dogs work on both sides of the handler and learn several directional cues including "go out," "get back," "get out," "get in," "hustle" and "easy." Everything is taught in a upbeat way, and the dogs soon take cues in motion.

With flatwork as a base to build on, Bond's novice class progresses to jumping. "Here, as in most aspects of agility, I adhere to the slogan, 'Go Low-Go Slow' in the early teaching phase," Bond says. He begins with low jumps in a straight line and varies the height, spacing, speed and approach angles as the dogs become ready.

To tame the tunnels, Bond begins with an open tunnel bunched together as tight as it will go. When a dog enjoys this short tunnel, the passageway is gradually opened and eventually curved. Once the dog understands the concept, it's easy to progress to the closed (collapsed) tunnel. Bond just gathers the fabric together so the obstacle resembles an open tunnel. Then he progressively lays out more fabric as the dog signals his readiness.

Introducing Obstacles in Order

Bond recommends that agility groups equip themselves with sturdy, fully adjustable contact obstacles that can go from lying flat on the ground to full competition height. When teaching the contact obstacles, he likes to begin big and wide and progress to small and narrow, so he starts with the A-frame. He lays it flat at first, then gradually increases the pitch and height when the dog's body language tells him he's ready.

Once a dog is at home on the wide, stable A-frame, Bond introduces the narrower dog walk. Again, the boards are laid flat on the ground and raised in small increments. Large dogs and dogs with poor body awareness often need extra help, so Bond lays a long ladder flat on the ground and has their handlers walk them through it. This exercise helps a dog become conscious

Adjustable obstacles are great if you can get them. This low dog walk sure beats having to lift Oliver onto a full-sized one and walk him down it.

of where his back legs are, increasing rear body awareness. If a dog still has trouble keeping his legs on the dog walk's narrow planks, Bond erects temporary side bars.

After a dog masters the dog walk, it is introduced to the see-saw, set at a low height. When novice dogs approach the see-saw they think it's another dog walk, as the approach to both obstacles looks the same at dog level. That's why Bond keeps the obstacle low and has the handler take it real slow until the dog learns the fulcrum and movement aspect of the obstacle.

A few years ago, when all obstacles were full height (before the newer ones were built to be adjustable), handlers introduced dogs to contact obstacles by lifting them halfway up the inclined planks and letting them walk back down, but this didn't work with frightened dogs and was back-breaking with big dogs. Today, Bond is pleased with the success his students have using lures (treats and/or toys) on adjustable contact obstacles. "The dogs learn much faster now because they have control over where they put their bodies," he explains.

After the dogs are accustomed to the obstacles, weave pole training and handling strategy round out Bond's novice class. "Remember," he says, "agility is a progression. Spend time building the foundation. Don't be in a hurry to go full height and full speed. Walk before you start running and you'll reap the benefits for a long time."

Additional Help for New Training Groups

Here are additional recommendations from Bond for those forming agility groups without the benefit of an experienced instructor:

- Take full advantage of the existing knowledge pool. Read books and articles on agility and surf the Internet. A lot of knowledgeable people are willing to help and advise. Just remember: What works for one dog-and-handler team may not work for another, and no one knows your dog as well as you do. So use the methods that feel right to you and discard the others.

- Go to seminars or bring trainers to your group. Again, keep the good and throw out any techniques that make you or your dog uncomfortable.

- When visiting an area with an established agility club or school, make arrangements to be a guest at a class.

ALL THAT EQUIPMENT

If you decide to form your own training group, you'll need a set of obstacles. You may decide to build some and buy others.

Agility Equipment Catalogs

Action K9 Sports, 27425 Cataluna Circle, Sun City, CA 92585, (909) 679-3699

Grateful Dog Agility Gear, 20146 Acre St., Winnetka, CA 91306, (818) 709-3510

MAX 200, 114 Beach St., Bldg. 5, Rockaway, NJ 07866, (800) 446-2920

On Course, P.O. Box 463, Branchville, NJ 07826, (800) 942-5216 or (201) 948-5691

Paw Z Tracks, Box 39, Site 1, RR #7, Calgary, Alberta, Canada T2P 2G7, (403) 248-8744

Pipe Dreams, 35 Walnut St., Turner Falls, MA 01376, (413) 863-8303

TD Agility Equip, 2949 Quince St. SE, Olympia, WA 98501, (360) 357-6722

Woulf-Fab, N1750 Buchanan Rd., Kaukauna, WI 54130, (414) 788-6706

Pipe Tunnels

West of the Rockies: ABC Peabody, P.O. Box 2928, Grand Junction, CO 81502, (970) 242-3664

East of the Rockies: ABC Peabody, P.O. Box 711, Warsaw, Indiana 47581, (219) 267-5166

Schauenberg, P.O. Box 335, Clifton, CO 81520, (970) 434-5134

Roberta Whitesides, 16025 W. 135th St., Lemont, IL 60439, (630) 257-5535

Cheap Practice Tunnels

Flaghouse, (800) 793-7900

IKEA, (800) 661-9807, $20 to $30

Toys-R-Us, stores nationwide, $16

U.S. Toy Company, (800) 448-4115, $49.95

Chute Tunnels

TX Canvas Products, 728 S. Beltline Rd., Irving, TX 75060, (214) 790-1501

PVC Fittings

Genova Products, (800) 521-7488

United States Plastics Corp., (800) 537-9724

Agility Equipment Plans

Agility Training, The Fun Sport For All Dogs, by Jane Simmons-Moake, Howell Book House, New York

Do-It-Yourself Plans for Agility Obstacles, Jim Hutchins, HOGA Agility, 128 Chippewa Circle, Jackson, MS 39211-6513

Fundamentals of Course Design for Dog Agility, by Stuart Mah, Clean Run Productions

USDAA Equipment Plans: P.O. Box 850955, Richardson, TX 75085-0995, (214) 231-9700

AKC Equipment Specs: 5580 Centerview Dr., Suite 200, Raleigh, NC 27606, (919) 233-9767

Course Measuring Wheels

Course Equipment and Supplies, (800) 942-5216

Action K9 Sports, 27425 Cataluna, Sun City, CA 92585, (909) 679-3699

Northern Pros & HandyMan, (800) 533-5545

Agility Course Design Magnetic Template Set

Deanna Avery, 22 Primrose Crescent, Brampton, Ontario, Canada L6Z 1E2, $35.

- Go to trials without your dog for an excellent learning experience. It will allow you to truly concentrate. Watch how the dog-handler teams work through problems, sequences and challenges on the course.

- Come back from trials or seminars and set personal and class goals with your group. Decide what style(s) of agility you will do and if you will work toward competition or hold only fun classes. Match your equipment to the style of agility you choose.

- Work as a group think tank. Sometimes a fresh set of eyes or a different approach can solve problems that may stymie an individual handler.

- Videotape your practices, training sessions and trial work. Then sit down with the tape and evaluate your handling and your dog's performance. Study the tape yourself first, then play it for your group and discuss it. Be brutally honest with yourself. You can only improve if you analyze you and your dog's shortcomings as well as your strengths.

Then correct your weaknesses and build on your strengths.

- Lay a good foundation. Progress to the next level of difficulty only when the concept is solid and you and your dog have attained confidence.

- Finally, to borrow a phrase from the Nike company, Just Do It! Agility is about running, jumping and playing with your dog. We all have a tendency to overanalyze all parts of this sport. Just get together with a group of people who want to have fun with their dogs and do it.

CONDITIONING YOUR TEAM

Agility dogs are athletes and athletes do their best when they are in top condition. And even though the human half of an agility team doesn't have to jump, weave and scramble over obstacles, you'll get around the course easier and direct Beau more smoothly if you have muscle tone, too. You and Beau can get into shape together and have fun doing it. Conditioning isn't hard but it is important. In fact, it's so important that I asked Mike Bond to help you again. Besides being an agility instructor and judge, he's been active in a variety of athletic events all his life.

Jean walks Annie and Bandit to loosen them up before working the obstacles.

"Conditioning is a combination of cardiovascular work, strength work, speed work, flexibility and weight control," says Bond. "Handlers often think they conditioned their dog when all they did was cut back on the dog's food until the dog lost some weight. All they have is a thinner, out of shape dog."

According to Bond, conditioning takes months and there are no short-cuts. You'll see external evidence of weight loss and muscle tone rather quickly, but the heart, lung, muscle, bone, tendon and ligament changes necessary for the stresses of heavy work and competition take much longer. Muscles must be toned, tendons and ligaments strengthened and excess weight gradually removed. The best way is to start slow, be patient and consistent, and gradually increase the physical demands as your canine athlete is ready for them. Take it especially easy if you have a puppy. Balance the physical stresses with the youngster's level of physical maturity.

Most dogs don't get enough of a workout running in the backyard, according to Bond, who says the best exercise for cardiovascular training is walking. He recommends starting slow after a vet's and an M.D.'s okay (remember, both members of the team need conditioning), and gradually increasing your distance. As you and your dog's base level of cardiovascular fitness develops, start trotting or jogging. Throw in changes of pace—even sprinting for short periods if you can. This develops different fibers within the same muscles. Your dog will think it's great if you make a game of it ("Come on, chase me") and keep it fun.

Always begin your conditioning program or your agility training sessions at a slow walk. Prevent injury by warming up cold muscles thoroughly before performing any physical activity.

For strength training, Bond recommends hill or stair work. It builds the strong front and rear quarters needed for the explosiveness of jumping and landing, as well as for climbing. He suggests making a game of it by encouraging your dog to play tag up a hill or having a training partner hide a treat or toy at the top of a hill or flight of stairs. Throwing a ball or toy up a hill and rewarding your dog with a treat and praise when he brings it back also works well if your dog is an eager retriever. Start slow and gradually build up the number of repetitions.

Bond also makes speed conditioning fun. He says retrieving a ball, Frisbee or favorite toy helps dogs develop acceleration abilities and allows them to stretch out, putting their bodies through a full and extended range of motion. Dogs that don't enjoy retrieving can gain speed through long recalls.

Have a training partner hold your dog while you go to the opposite end of the yard or training area. Then open your arms, call your dog and take a few steps backward so your dog will come even faster. Hug him when he arrives and give him a treat. Then do it again. Sprint chase games with changes of direction also work well, but only if you are in shape to run and change directions safely.

While working on cardiovascular training, strength and speed, Bond also conditions for flexibility. He recommends starting with a series of stretching exercises, gently flexing and extending each of your dog's legs. Spinal flexes and extensions come next. Do them by bending your dog slowly around your legs. Also, praise your dog when he play bows or arches his back and he will soon do these natural spinal stretches more often.

Don't forget that humans should stretch before and after physical activity, too. A variety of stretches beneficial to handlers can be found at your local library. Look for them in any good yoga book. "Just remember," says Bond, "don't bounce on a stretch. Let your own body weight stretch your muscles, tendons and ligaments."

Cavaletti jumping (a series of low jumps) is part of Bond's formula to build strength, speed and flexibility. He starts with very low heights in a straight line jumping chute (jumps with a barrier on both sides). Then he gradually bends the chute into an arc in both directions so the dogs learn to bend left and right. Eventually the jumping chute is formed into a circle and the dogs run it both clockwise and counterclockwise, allowing them to flex in motion from both sides of the spine. According to Bond, this helps to minimize a dog favoring his strong side.

Another conditioning exercise Bond recommends is called a "cone drill." The dog-and-handler team target to a series of pylons and walk, trot or run to them executing a turn or spin or lead change (depending on their speed) around each one. This helps stretch out the dog and the handler and makes a wonderful warm-up exercise.

Throughout his conditioning program, Bond still works on agility, concentrating on obstacle discrimination, directional control, distance control and sequencing. He keeps the jumps low, gradually working up to full height several weeks before the next competition. "I like a little more repetition to work through any problems," he says. "If I repeatedly have dogs jump at regulation height, I'll start to see signs of physical breakdown from fatigue over time and I won't get in enough repetitions to work through the sequences. I like to pace them."

TRANSITION TIME

One of these days Beau will be able to perform all the obstacles he needs for a novice course, and if you're as eager to enter the ring as most agility competitors, you'll see competition as only a step away. Fortunately, that's not the case. Fortunately, because even though it would make things faster, performing one obstacle at a time would never culminate in one of agility's most rewarding features—teamwork with your dog.

Teamwork develops during the transition period between learning each obstacle as a separate entity and running entire courses. During this transition, Beau will learn to hustle from one obstacle to another at your signal, and both of you will perfect your timing. Agility courses are seldom the same twice, but after you and Beau learn to read each other's body language, challenging courses will add to your fun. Sure you'll expect the unexpected on every new course, but you'll also handle it with ease.

If Beau had an ideal introduction to the obstacles, he knows each one by name and can negotiate it from either side of you. But if you always worked Beau off the same side, or haven't given each obstacle a name, you can still correct those deficiencies during the transition period.

The transition period is critical to your agility success, so I asked agility judge John Loomis and his wife Patricia how they present it to their students. They're the owner-instructors of Alibi Kennel and Training facility, and you met them earlier in this chapter. Here are their suggestions.

Straight-Line Sequencing

As soon as Beau obeys basic obedience commands and is comfortable with all the agility equipment, it's time to make the transition to straight-line sequencing. That's agility jargon for performing two or more obstacles in order. It's the essential step between doing one obstacle at a time and running the entire course.

Besides teaching Beau to move from one obstacle to the next on command, straight-line sequence training will teach him to discriminate between obstacles if he hasn't already learned their names. It's also a good time for you to review the names you gave each obstacle, until they are as familiar as your own name. It may have been easy to remember each name when you worked

OBEDIENCE FOR AGILITY DOGS

There is nothing wrong with introducing the agility obstacles before Beau obeys obedience commands, but you won't be able to progress to off-lead work unless he always comes when called and trots along beside you without running off. Every good agility dog also responds to the "sit" and "down" commands instantly, even when the dog is some distance from his handler. Staying in position when told and responding to your first cue or command are also prerequisites for earning titles. If you have to tell Beau twice, an obstacle may be missed.

Who are these well-trained dogs? They are Holly, Lilly, Scud, Reece and Dallas and they are posing in Switzerland, where they represented the United States at the World Agility Championship in 1996. Top agility dogs have some obedience training, too.

Where can Beau learn these skills? He can learn them at obedience school, or even at home if you use a good training book. But school is the best choice for a number of reasons. At obedience school Beau will get used to obeying commands amid the distractions of new people, strange dogs and a variety of noises—kind of like the setting of an agility trial. Concentrating despite distractions is one of the keys to success in agility. You'll realize its importance the first time someone's dog loses sight of his handler and runs the wrong way on the agility course. Upon leaving the ring, the handler will invariably say, "But he always does it right at home." And you know what? It's true. The dog probably does it just fine in a familiar place with no distractions. But that doesn't help him at an agility trial. So attend obedience classes if you can, in a different setting than where Beau does agility. The training will make Beau a more reliable agility dog and a better companion.

Some commands that help agility dogs, such as "wait" and "easy," and directional aids like "left" and "right," are not included in typical novice obedience courses. However, once you learn dog training basics and Beau responds to your commands, you'll be able to teach them to him yourself. Ask your obedience or agility instructor if you need help introducing them. Then teach the commands in a different location from where you do agility.

Beau on one obstacle and then moved on to the next, but now you are going to have to call them out quickly and correctly. "Don't confuse your dog by calling different obstacles by the same name, or by calling the same obstacle by different names," Patricia Loomis cautions. "We found that using 'jump' for all the hurdles is okay, but we use 'over' for the broad jump. It doesn't matter what name you give an obstacle as long as you call it the same thing every time. Don't say 'tunnel' one day, 'under' the next and 'go in, go in' when you get excited. Be consistent with your commands."

Although the Loomises train their dogs to work from either side and well away from them right from the beginning, they agree that if you haven't done it yet, now is the time. During straight-line sequencing you can teach Beau to work off your right side as well as your left, and gradually increase the distance between you.

Sequence One

As the first sequence, the Loomises recommend two jumps in a straight line around 25 feet apart (20 feet is sufficient if Beau is small). Set their height lower than Beau is used to so he can concentrate on sequencing without worrying about how to execute the jumps. With Beau on-lead, introduce him to the sequence by running by the hurdles while he jumps over them.

Excite him with upbeat talk just before you start and praise him when he finishes. He'll love it.

Timing your agility commands is critical in competition, but it will be second nature by then if you start practicing now. The Loomises recommend giving the second jump command while Beau is still soaring over the first jump. And, if you are calling Beau's name before every command ("Beau, hup!"), stop before it becomes a habit. In competition, when the obstacles are close together and Beau is cruising through the course at top speed, even his one syllable name takes too long to say.

How long should you practice the sequence of two low jumps on-lead? Until Beau works confidently on either side of you and understands that he is supposed to take two jumps in a row with no hesitation; and until timing your commands comes easily to you.

Out of everything you have to remember, what's most important? Having fun. Beau won't receive his reward until the end of a sequence, so give him a big hug and occasionally a treat or toy following every successful series.

When you and Beau are ready, the next step is performing the sequence off-lead. Did Beau still do the sequence easily with you on either side? Then gradually raise the jumps to competitive height while progressively reducing the space between them to 15 feet. No matter how well Beau does, take nothing for granted. Always give the command for the second jump (and later the third and fourth jumps) while Beau is in midair, and follow every sequence with profuse praise.

Sequence Two

When Beau breezes through a sequence of two jumps at competitive height off lead, it's time to add a third hurdle. Lower all three jumps, spread them to 25 feet apart, put Beau on-lead and work him on either side of you as before. Then gradually work your way off-lead and back to competitive height with a 15-foot spread. According to Pat Loomis, one way to add zest to training sessions is to throw a ball over a straight line of hurdles, then send Beau after it. Use the command "go out" or "go on" when you want Beau to work a line of jumps out ahead of you.

Varying Your Sequences

When Beau easily takes three hurdles off-lead at competition height and distance, add a tunnel to your sequence. When do you give the next command to a dog inside a tunnel? Give it the instant Beau's head emerges from the exit. Sometimes place the tunnel at the beginning of the three-jump sequence and other times put it at the end. "Don't pattern train," Pat Loomis cautions (that's agility jargon for setting up sequences or courses the same way all the time). "All agility courses are different, and setting up creative sequences gives you the opportunity to teach your dog to expect change and look to you for guidance around the course."

Correcting Mistakes

What if Beau refuses a jump or tries to go around an obstacle? "We recommend the circle correction," Pat Loomis says. "Instead of calling your dog to you, which could lead to back-jumping (that's agility jargon for jumping an obstacle in the wrong direction), call your dog to your side as you move in a circle, clockwise if the dog was on your left or counterclockwise if you were handling off your right side. Then use your left or right hand (depending on which side Beau is on) to signal the missed obstacle.

"All dogs miss or refuse an obstacle once in a while, and this technique works as well in competition as it does in practice. But if your dog misses or refuses often, you may have moved ahead too quickly. Lower the jumps, spread the obstacles and use your lead. Build Beau's confidence, perfect your timing and you'll soon be ready to add more obstacles."

Pause Table Time

After Beau successfully performs three jumps at full height 15 feet apart and effortlessly starts or finishes the series with a tunnel, it's time to stir a pause table into your recipe for sequential success. Begin by selecting a command for the table (if you haven't already) and use it every time. Then lower the jumps and start with only two hurdles and a low pause table. Let Beau see you place a toy or treat on the pause table, then send him to the table and run there beside him the first few times. Soon he should be raring to go to the table without you. If he is hesitant anyway, Pat Loomis suggests having someone stand behind the pause table. After you send Beau, they should show him his treat or toy while calling him.

Once Beau handles the pause table happily, add more hurdles, one at a time. Raise their height slowly, and gradually bring them closer together until he jumps several hurdles 15 feet apart at competitive height and goes to the pause table by himself. "This is a very good exercise if you don't do it too often," Loomis says. "Too much repetition may cause your dog to go to the

Bud Kramer, founder of NCDA (now UKC) agility, performs an exciting sequence with his dog, Fancee.

table every time he sees the table. This is also a good time to start practicing running by several obstacles without sending Beau to any of them. It will teach him that he shouldn't automatically perform every obstacle in front of him."

Making Your Sequences Exciting

When Beau zips through straight-line sequences with jumps and a pause table, bring back the tunnel. Now mix and match so the tunnel is first one day and last another day and the pause table appears between the jumps sometimes and follows the tunnel other times. After Beau masters these sequences, gradually add contact obstacles such as the dog walk, A-frame and finally, the weave poles. "Never rush your dog," Pat Loomis cautions. "If you get into trouble, go back to lower heights and longer distances between obstacles, and use your lead if you need to. You're building a foundation, so take all the time you and your dog need to make it solid."

The Transition to Turns

Does Beau perform a variety of straight-line sequences off-lead, with you handling from either side? Then he's ready to learn turns.

To teach the right turn, set up two low jumps in a straight line and put two more low jumps off to the right at a 90-degree angle. There should be at least 20 to 25 feet between them. You will usually handle Beau from your left side when you ask for a right turn, so teach this sequence with him on your left. Send Beau over the first two jumps and, while he is in midair, use the command "come" or "right." As Beau turns toward you, use your regular jump command to send him over the third and fourth jumps. Progress gradually as before, raising the heights to competitive level and reducing the distance between the jumps to 15 feet. You can add any number of obstacles in a variety of sequences as long as you take your time and go back a few steps if Beau seems confused.

Since most dogs aren't as comfortable working on the handler's right side, the Loomises use a different method when teaching the left turn. Instead of creating a 90-degree angle, they set up three low jumps in an arc with 20 feet between them. The arc makes for a smoother transition. Prepare Beau to take the low jumps counterclockwise by working him on-lead from your right side. Each time he is in the air over a jump, repeat the command "left" or "come." The instant he responds by turning toward you, give the next jump command. After practicing a few times, try it off-lead.

As Beau becomes comfortable with the turn, gradually raise the jumps and reduce the distance between them. During left or right turns, use the same command consistently and always reward with lots of praise. If Beau refuses a jump, correct with the circle technique.

An Occasional Course

Once Beau has perfected sequences with left and right turns, your reward is running entire courses, right? Sorry, but it's time to practice patience again. "Don't work entire courses with your dog for a long time, and then do it only occasionally," Pat Loomis recommends. "Smaller sequences, carefully planned to build control and speed, are much more effective than running entire courses."

PREPARING FOR COMPETITION

Before entering a trial, you and Beau should master sequences containing a variety of challenges. In agility jargon, a challenge is a place on the course where your dog could easily make a mistake such as taking the wrong obstacle, or where you should perform a handling maneuver such as switching sides. If you are in an agility class, your instructor is probably already setting up more difficult sequences as you and Beau demonstrate your ability to handle them. But if you have formed your own agility group, you'll have to create sequences with appropriate challenges to help each other get ready for competition. Keep them simple at first, and add difficulty gradually.

Examples of challenges are S curves on the course where a simple side-switch keeps you on the shortest track. Make the switch smoothly by crossing behind (never in front of) Beau. While you don't have to change sides, deciding not to means taking the long way around the obstacles and having to run faster than Beau just to keep up with him.

CHAPTER 5

AGILITY *Events*

When you're satisfied with Beau's practice runs and ready to try the real thing, here's how to enter and prepare for events.

To enter AKC, UKC or USDAA events, you'll need a recent copy of their publications. AKC's coming events are published in the *Events Calendar* supplement to the *AKC Gazette*. The UKC's magazine *Bloodlines* will keep you up to date on UKC trials and the USDAA announces its events in its publication, *USDAA Dog Agility Report*. (For more information on the agility organizations and their publications, see the Appendix.)

When you find a trial you want to enter, write to the contact person listed for that event (usually the trial secretary) and ask for an entry form. Along with it, you will receive a premium list or flyer with additional information, including directions to the trial site and motels in the area that accept dogs. There will also be a deadline for sending in entries. Take it seriously, because there are no exceptions.

After you fill in your entry form and return it with the correct fee, you'll receive a confirmation of your entry. It will include the number of dogs entered in each class, what time the trial starts and Beau's entry number. That number will be on the armband you will receive at the trial and wear when competing.

EVENT INFORMATION ON THE INTERNET

If you have access to the Internet, you can get up-to-date event information from the following Web sites.

AKC   www.akc.org

Locate AKC agility event listings by selecting **Dogs In Competition** from the choices on the AKC Home page. Then select **Events & Awards Search.** Even without knowing or entering the event name, you can, and should, narrow your search as much as possible by selecting either the state, or the time range you're interested in, or both. Select **Agility Trials** from the Competition Type pop-up window and then select **Event Search**. You'll get the name of the club hosting the event, the event's location, dates and closing dates for registration. By selecting the name of the club, you'll get all the contact information you need.

UKC   www.ukcdogs.com

To find UKC event listings, select **U.K.C. Events,** found on the Home page, then select **Upcoming Events.** Scroll down to the bottom of that page to **Seminars, conformation, obedience, agility, total dog** and select it, then finally, select **Performance Events Only.** From here you can select the month you're interested in and go directly to it, or you can scroll through all of the events which are listed chronologically. Use the agility events symbol (an A-frame) to guide you to the events that are agility only or agility and obedience combined.

USDAA   www.usdaa.com

Retrieve contact information for USDAA events by selecting **Event Calendar** on the Home page menu. Scroll down through the dates and locations of events until you find the one that you're interested in. (This information is listed chronologically.) Then follow the provided link for who to contact. Most links will lead you to the Affiliated Groups page. Select the geographic area for the event you want to attend—be sure to remember the name of the club that is hosting the event so that you get the correct contact information!

PRETRIAL ANXIETY

Pretrial anxiety affects everyone differently. For many it's cumulative, beginning with a flutter of apprehension when you send in your entry and building through the next couple of weeks as you practice with your dog and pack your vehicle. If Beau feels your tension, it could put a damper on his performance or even make him lose his appetite, adding yet another complication to your growing list of worries. The night before the trial you may sleep fitfully, if at all. Then you hit the road, gulping coffee and driving white-knuckled, agonizing over whether you left something essential at home and whether you will get lost on the way to the trial. Top this off with stage fright at ringside and it's no mystery why you and Beau may not perform as well at a trial as you did in practice.

But it doesn't have to be that way. With just a little advance planning you can alleviate most anxieties, leaving only stage fright to contend with—and we'll contend with it later.

PLANNING YOUR TRIP

Begin trial preparations at least a week before your trip. First, get out your road atlas and a yellow transparent marker and figure out the best route to the trial, using turnpikes and major highways whenever possible. If it's a long drive, check the time zones so you don't pass through one and lose an hour without realizing it.

Estimate traveling time by using the mileage chart in your atlas. Then add an extra two hours as a safety margin. Few things jangle the nerves like encountering a long detour or becoming muddled in a strange metropolis and frantically searching for the trial site. Give yourself the extra time even if you are a seasoned traveler and know exactly where you're going. Beau is new at this and may become carsick, necessitating a dog and crate clean-up, or both of you may be nervous and need to make more potty stops than usual. Besides, an unhurried feeling gives you a sense of well being on the way to the trial. It's good to know you will arrive with plenty of time to warm up and get Beau accustomed to the area.

If you own a recreational vehicle, camping at the trial site the night before the event will alleviate worries about making it on time. When an agility trial is held in conjunction with a dog show, the grounds are filled with hundreds of campers, giving you an opportunity to make friends with dog show and obedience exhibitors as well as agility competitors. If you don't own a camper but dread the hassle of setting out before dawn, try arriving the evening before and staying at a nearby motel. Check your premium list (the information that came along with your entry form) for motels that accept dogs, and reserve early. Mention that you are with the dog show or agility trial (sometimes a discount has been arranged) and get a confirmation number. When you arrive, find the trial site before you settle in for the night so you won't have to worry about which way to turn in the morning. Then ask for a wake-up call, set your own alarm clock just in case, and have a relaxing evening.

Planned Packing

Lists will also help alleviate anxiety if you start them about a week before the event. Major headings could be Take, Do and Buy. The box on the next page has an example of some items that might go on your lists.

A different format may work better for you. For example, if your children are going to the trial too, you will have to pack for them. Make your lists detailed to the point of describing the clothing. If you just write "two outfits," you'll still be running around deciding what to pack at the last minute and could forget something.

Dog food and water from home should always be on your list. Unfamiliar water and the dog food samples often distributed at events could upset Beau's stomach. It's much safer to let him try new foods a little at a time at home.

Agility trials are held in all kinds of weather, so select clothing that can be layered. It's not unusual to start the day shivering in the morning dew with temperatures in the 40s and swelter in 85-degree heat by early afternoon. Also, take rain gear to every trial, no matter what the forecast.

Once you make your lists, you'll probably think of more items over the next few days. Jot them down as soon as they come to mind and you won't forget them. Just before you load your vehicle, sit down and reread your lists slowly. Visualize the road trip, the agility event and staying in your recreational vehicle or a motel, if applicable. Do you have everything you need to complete your morning ritual? If you can't think of anything to add, rest assured that any item left behind won't be vital. Check off items from the list as you load them in your vehicle. When each one has been checked off, you have alleviated the worry of forgetting something important.

Take

Me	**Beau**
Red striped shirt	Two dishes
New khaki pants	Dog food and treats
Red belt	Gallon jug of water
White sneakers	Crate and blanket
Socks	Brush
Underwear	Collar
Pjs	Lead
Toiletries	Poop scooper
Entry confirmation	Heartworm tab
Rain gear	Toys and chews
Alarm clock	
Folding chair	

Do

Bathe Beau and flea dip if needed

Trim Beau's toenails

Gas up the van or car

Check oil, tires, water, belts and hoses

Buy

Soda and snacks

Dog treats

KEEPING BEAU SAFE AND COMFORTABLE ON THE ROAD

Do the words, "Wanna go for a ride?" send Beau into a toe-tapping dance of glee? Is he content and happy in your vehicle, even on long trips? Or is he reluctant to get into the car because road trips make him nervous or carsick? Perhaps all your car trips together have been brief. If so, you don't know how he reacts on long trips. It's not a good idea to wait until your first agility trial, 100 miles away, to find out. You may be in for several messy surprises and Beau may arrive feeling anything but agile.

If Beau relaxes during long rides, that's lucky for both of you. But if he's an anxious traveler or if long rides make him carsick (some dogs froth at the mouth instead of vomiting when they suffer motion sickness), then starting from scratch may change his attitude and settle his tummy. Before making your first attitude-adjusting trip, Beau needs a suitcase, just like any other traveler. What goes in Beau's suitcase? He does. Beau's suitcase is called a dog crate.

Why Crates are Great

Modern dogs' ancestors spent much of their time in the relative security of their den. That's why it will take only a brief period of adjustment until Beau feels comfortable and protected in a dog crate. Dog crates aren't cruel, as some people imagine. Instead, they have saved dogs' lives, much like car seats have saved human infants.

Besides making travel safer, dog crates are also useful for housebreaking, essential when staying in a motel with your dog and convenient at agility trials. You know how children, when they want something, tend to say, "Everybody else has one." Well, it's true about dog crates, too. Every agility competitor really does have one (or two, if they have two dogs).

Buy Beau a crate that's large enough for him to stand up and turn around in easily. If he isn't full grown, take that into consideration and buy a crate big enough to be useful all his life. Bedding on the bottom of the crate will make it soft and snug. Use material that's easy to clean or change in the event of a mishap, and isn't dangerous if Beau chews or swallows some of it. For example, several layers of newspaper (black and white, not color like the Sunday comics) make good, disposable bedding until Beau gets over his car sickness. For extra coziness, rip one newspaper section into long, thin streamers and place them in the crate on top of the whole sections. Carry extra paper

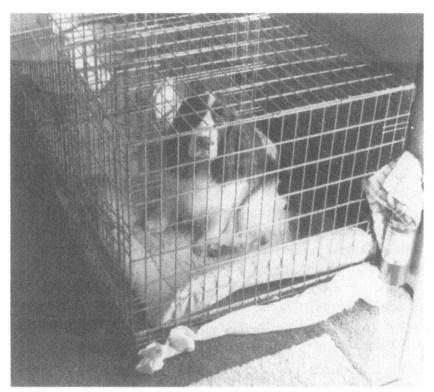

Duchess relaxes on a soft pad in her crate in Marilyn's motor home. The old blanket beneath the crate keeps the carpet from getting damaged by the crate's metal bottom.

along while you are desensitizing Beau (see "Road-Tripping 101"). After Beau becomes a tranquil (not tranquilized) traveler, put something more permanent on the floor of his crate. Washable pillows, cushions or carpet samples all make a comfortable bed for a crated dog.

If Beau has never been crated, he should get used to his crate in your home before taking a ride in it. Put the crate in the kitchen or any room that gets lots of traffic and let Beau get used to seeing it for a few hours. Then toss his favorite toy or treat in the crate ahead of him, say "crate" and, as gently as possible (but as firmly as you have to), put Beau in and shut the door. Then walk out of the room. Don't wait around to see how Beau will react, because that will entice him to react. Instead, be casual and matter-of-fact and he may take his cue from you and settle in. Every time you put Beau in his crate, throw a goodie in ahead of him. Soon he will learn the word "crate" and enter it himself, without your help.

Beau may cry the first few times he is introduced to his crate, but if you walk away and don't take him out of the crate until he settles down, he'll soon learn to like it. If he takes longer than four days to stop complaining in his crate, make a sudden loud noise from another room such as stamping your foot or slapping the wall as soon as he whines or barks. But don't yell or say anything. It's best if Beau thinks that his own clamor, not you, caused the noise. As soon as he vocalizes again, make your sharp noise again and repeat as often as necessary.

If all else fails, fill an inexpensive water pistol (not a high-powered one) with cool tap water and wait in another room. When Beau makes a racket, walk in silently and squirt him one time, through the crate door, full in the face. Then leave again. As soon as he is quiet for a few minutes, go to him without the water pistol and pet and praise him. Repeat as necessary. It won't be necessary for long.

Whatever you do, don't give in and take Beau out of his crate to stop his protests. That's exactly what he wants, so he will feel rewarded for complaining loudly. Wait until he is quiet for at least a minute before going to him and letting him out.

Road-Tripping 101

Once Beau is happy in his crate, it's time to introduce him to car rides in it. If he's been in a car before he may have strong feelings, either positive or negative, about his traveling experiences. Have all his previous rides terminated in vaccinations at the veterinary clinic? Then he might have made an association between car rides and needles and became an anxious traveler. Have Beau's outings included playing in the park, agility lessons or visits to friends' houses? Then his reaction to riding may range from indifferent to enthusiastic. Even dogs that love going for a ride may suffer motion sickness on long trips, but dogs that worry about going some place scary are at a distinct disadvantage.

To make sure your Beau is never at a disadvantage, create a tie-down system in your vehicle so his crate can't slide or roll over on curves or quick stops. Bungee cords are easy to attach and work well in many cars and vans. Position the crate so it receives air flow, and if Beau can see you, that's a plus.

Long before entering a distant agility trial, begin taking Beau along with you on a variety of errands. When possible, take him for a short walk or play with him at your destination, but even if the trip is strictly business, like a

VENTILATION IS VITAL

The temperature inside your vehicle, even when it is parked in the shade, is usually 25 or more degrees hotter than outside the vehicle. That means when you are comfortable in 75-degree weather outside your car, your dog could die in 100-degree heat while waiting inside the vehicle. Every year hundreds of pets die from being left in closed cars for just a few minutes.

It's best not to leave Beau alone inside your car at all, but if you must, make sure the car is in the shade. Don't put the windows down so low that he could squeeze out, but do keep them low enough on both sides to provide plenty of ventilation. Also, when driving with the air-conditioner on and a crated dog in the back of your vehicle, check occasionally to make sure the air is reaching your dog.

Never take equipment for granted. A modern, upscale motor home recently became a death trap for several show dogs. The owner was showing one dog and thought her other dogs were resting comfortably inside the air-conditioned vehicle. No one realized that the air-conditioner had quit, because the generator was still humming along. Six dogs died from the heat.

quick ride to the post office, it will help Beau get used to traveling and give you an opportunity to evaluate his tolerance for road trips.

If Beau becomes carsick on any of your routine trips, notice how long that ride was, as it may have stretched the limits of his motion tolerance. Then build up his tolerance by taking several trips just under his limit, before gradually extending his time on the road. Also make note of how long before his ride he ate or drank. Some dogs ride best on an empty stomach, while others are helped by a couple of dry dog biscuits a half hour or so before they travel. Experiment, and you'll soon discover what works for Beau. In the meantime, he may outgrow his motion sickness or it may simply disappear when he realizes that most trips don't end in scary places.

OFF TO THE TRIAL

You're packed, Beau's been walked and crated, it's early enough so you don't have to hurry and you're off to the agility trial. Play your favorite music or an audio book and enjoy the ride.

But what if you're feeling fuzzy from not sleeping well last night? Take an aspirin if they agree with you. For some reason, they clear the cobwebs from the brain. Even without an aspirin, you'll be alert soon enough. It's going to be an amazing day, full of learning experiences and new acquaintances.

There are two types of travelers: those who stop at every rest area and scenic view and those whose highest praise for a trip is, "We made good time." While you don't have to be as extreme as the former, neither you nor Beau will make good time where it counts, on the agility course, if you arrive stiff from sitting too long without a break. If the trip takes under an hour, go for it all at once (unless Beau needs a break to prevent car sickness). But if it takes longer, stop once an hour so you and Beau can stretch your legs. Look out for cactus, thistles, briar bushes and anything else that might hurt Beau's pads, and wherever you walk, always pick up after him. A full five minutes of walking every hour is enough to keep you both limber, but count it as 10 minutes when figuring your trip time. That allows for parking, finding the dog walking area and using the facilities.

As you near the agility trial, look for signs pointing your way to the site (they may say DOG SHOW), but don't count on them. It takes many volunteers to run a dog event, and sometimes no one gets around to putting up directional signs.

There may be parking attendants at the entrance to the trial site. If there are, show them your exhibitor's pass or anything you received in the mail after sending in your entry. You'll probably have to pay for parking anyway, but sometimes exhibitors pay less than spectators. When agility is held in conjunction with a dog show, there may be well over 2,000 dogs on the grounds and many separate judging rings, so it's helpful if you can park close to the agility ring. The parking attendant may be able to tell you where it is.

ARRIVING AND CHECKING IN

It may have been an empty exhibition hall or a vacant fairgrounds yesterday, but the day of a dog event it's a bustling and crowded canine city. Vendors sell the latest in canine health and beauty items, handlers groom show dogs to perfection, friends who haven't seen each other since their last dog event catch up on each other's news, and an air of expectation electrifies the area.

Did you attend a few agility events without your dog? Then you probably know what to expect. But unless Beau previously competed in a different dog activity, such as obedience, it's all going to be new to him. You're

ICE IS NICE

It's a good idea to carry a bag of ice in a cooler for summer agility trials. Put a few ice cubes in your dog's bowl on a hot afternoon and he'll be as tickled as a kid with a Popsicle. Licking ice is good for him, too. It cools him off slowly without bloating him the way gulping too much water can.

In addition to bagged ice, it's smart to carry a couple of "crate conditioners." Make them a few days before the trial by filling two-liter or two-quart plastic bottles three-quarters full of water, capping them and freezing them solid. Giant breeds will appreciate gallon jugs and half-liter bottles are best for tiny dogs.

Frozen crate conditioners will stay fairly solid for up to two days in your cooler, and can be placed inside the crate to cool your dog during the hottest hours of a July afternoon. After they melt they are still useful. A bit of water of any temperature feels good on a dog's warm underbelly. In fact, pouring some water right into the crate will help cool your dog if your vehicle ever breaks down on a muggy day with no help in sight.

early, right? Then take him for a walk and introduce him to the area. Let him look around and sniff for a few minutes and watch his reaction. If he's curious but happy, wander over to the agility ring. That way Beau will get to see the area while you take care of business. Check in at the registration table or with the ring stewards (depending on the trial). Make sure Beau is entered in the correct jump-height class and pick up your armband. The armband will have your entry number printed on it and you will wear it on your upper left arm when competing.

If Beau seems nervous on his walk, make sure your vehicle is well ventilated and let him settle in his crate for a few minutes while you check in and get your armband. Then walk him around some more—starting at the perimeter of the agility area and gradually moving in closer as he relaxes. What if Beau is over-stimulated rather than nervous and wants to play with every person and dog he encounters? Check in without him, then take him on a long, brisk walk to help settle him. Eventually you, he, your comfortable folding chair and Beau's crate (if permitted at ringside), should end up at the agility ring.

Equipment Familiarization (The Warm Up That Isn't)

Although agility obstacles have to conform to the organization's regulations, they may look a little different than Beau is used to. Perhaps the wings on the hurdles are shaped like dogs or dinosaurs, or the tunnels are brightly colored while your practice tunnels are neutral.

Some, but not all, agility trials provide time before the actual course is laid out for handlers to introduce their dogs to the obstacles, one obstacle at a time. (Don't use this time to plan handling strategy or practice sequences at USDAA or AKC events, as the obstacles may not be in order.) Other trials allow equipment familiarization only with the contact obstacles. Check your rule book, as only one try per obstacle may be allowed, depending on the organization.

When checking in, ask if and when there will be an opportunity for a "warm-up." That's what many clubs call these sessions. (Beau will not really be warmed up after introducing him to the obstacles. Warm-ups for canine athletes and their handlers are covered later in this chapter.)

"Warm-up" time is limited, but Beau should try each obstacle, so help him feel confident by starting with the ones you think will be easiest for him.

Jamie Watters, 14, keeps her border collie Annie focused on the contact zone. Work the contacts on the trial equipment if you have the opportunity.

Reward with plenty of praise. Do the obstacles he breezes over just once and spend most of your allotted time helping him feel secure on the ones that make him wary (unless only one try per obstacle is allowed). Also, check the footing so you will know in advance if the contact obstacles or the ground is wet or slippery. Then handle accordingly when it's your turn in the ring.

Following equipment familiarization (if there is one), the obstacles will be laid out to create the agility course. Expect it to take an hour or so and use the time to keep Beau relaxed and happy. You know him best. Anything from snoozing in his crate to a long, slow walk around the grounds is fine. Just be back on time for the judge's briefing.

The Judge's Briefing
After the course is laid out and the obstacles are numbered, the judge will give it a final inspection and measure the course. Then he or she will talk to all the handlers at once, telling you the length of the course and the course time (how much time you have to complete the course before you will be faulted for going overtime) and anything else you need to know before you compete.

Course Familiarization or Where's My Map?
Handlers have an opportunity to walk the course without their dogs at USDAA, AKC and NADAC trials after the judge's briefing. At UKC trials they may take their dogs through the course on-lead. Chances are your heart was racing while the judge talked, but to get the most out of course familiarization you'll have to calm down enough to think straight. Taking a few deep breaths usually helps.

To be the best possible handler for Beau, you have to do two jobs during course familiarization. First, memorize the course (relying on the numbers placed on each obstacle during your run doesn't give you time to cue your dog). When memorizing, don't look at the course one obstacle at a time, but instead break it into sequences. Not only does thinking in sequences make the course easier to remember, but it makes it make sense.

Your second job is planning your handling strategy. Where should you switch sides? Where can you send Beau on ahead? Where will he need you right beside him to work a contact or avoid a trap? When should you be on a certain side of him to help him turn toward the correct obstacle? (Dogs tend to turn toward the side their handler is on, so be on his right if you want him to make a right turn and vice versa.) Decide in advance how you will

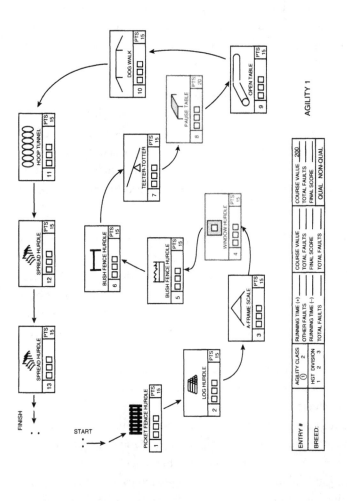

AGILITY 1

This is the layout of an actual UKC Agility 1 course, created and used at a trial by judge Dr. Mike Bond. Which side of your dog will you start on? If you switch sides, where will you do it? Will you do it again later in the course? Where could Beau take the wrong obstacle unless you direct him to the correct one in plenty of time? Could it happen more than once? Where should you be right beside him to work the contact zones?

These are among the decisions you will make during course familiarization, and they are part of what makes agility anything but boring.

Jean Carter teaches Bandit to go out in front of her and take an obstacle on command. Later she may use that move when planning her competitive strategy.

handle each sequence, but don't try any new moves. Sure, you'll see some handlers leave their dogs at the start line and call them through the first four obstacles, but if you never did it with Beau before, don't try it for the first time in competition. Instead, do what you practiced and work on new and better handling methods when you get home. Seeing what works and what doesn't for other handlers is an excellent way to learn.

If you watched an agility trial before entering, I bet you thought some handlers looked kind of funny when they crouched way down on the ground during course familiarization. Those same handlers probably made strange hand motions while their feet did a curious dance. They may have looked odd, but they were the smart handlers. They got down to their dog's eye level to see the course—with its traps and options—just as their dogs would see it, then practiced hand signals and footwork as if their dogs were with them. Try it. You'll be in good company with the other smart handlers. Acting out your strategy will improve your handling and help you memorize the course, and Beau's performance will reflect your smoothness and confidence.

Following course familiarization, go by the steward's table again. Find out when your jump-height class will start and if any of the dogs scheduled to go on before Beau are absent. When there are absentees and you don't know it, your turn will come earlier than you estimated and you and Beau may not be ready. If there are plenty of dogs before Beau, let him relax while you watch the competition. By your turn, you'll be able to run the course in your sleep. Just don't become so intent on the show that you forget the most important precompetition step of all: warming up your dog and yourself.

WARM-UP TIME

We all know that runners, race walkers, tennis players and all other athletes warm up before participating in their sport, but many agility handlers jump out of their vehicles after hours of sitting and immediately lift and carry heavy items such as dog crates and coolers. That done, they spend the next hour or two sitting at ringside. When it's finally their turn, it's like flipping a switch from "off" to "on" as they race around the course without even limbering up. Are they sore later? You bet. But sore muscles could be the least of their problems. Heavy exercise without a warm-up is an invitation to serious injury.

Learn by Watching Your Dog

Dogs, on the other hand, instinctively take better care of their bodies than people do. After napping in a crate, they enjoy a leisurely stretch before emerging. In fact, most animals stretch every time they get up or change position, which adds up to many times a day. Frequent stretching keeps their bodies in condition for action. So, instead of rushing to unload your vehicle when you arrive at an agility trial, borrow a bit of your dog's instinctive behavior. While Beau stretches, you stretch too. Yawning is a simple form of stretching if you do it as nature intended—big and wide with your arms above your head. Go ahead, try it. But don't stop there. Here's the personal warm-up strategy Mike Bond uses when he competes. It will make both you and Beau limber enough to handle the rigors of running the course.

Bond, the agility instructor, judge, exhibitor and former competitive athlete you met earlier, begins his pretrial routine at home by walking his dog to loosen its muscles (and his) before crating the dog for the trip. He gives himself enough time so that upon arrival he can potty his dog and take it on a slow walk for several minutes. Following the walk, Bond limbers up his dog with a few gentle stretching exercises. To increase lateral flexibility, he has the dog walk slowly around and between his legs and he also encourages it to play bow, which arches the dog's back and stretches its spine.

For his own warm-up, Bond does a few gentle stretches on the ground (found in any good yoga book). Following the stretches, he and his dog do light trotting and quick starts-and-stops to begin loading their muscles and lubricating their joints. A few play retrieves with a ball or the dog's favorite toy are next, following by weaving exercises, in which the dog becomes more supple by weaving in, out and around Bond's open-legged stance somewhat faster than before.

When there is still plenty of time before their turn, Bond takes his dog to the practice hurdle (at most agility trials, there will be a practice or warm-up hurdle near the agility ring). He sets it rather low at first, and gradually increases it to regulation height. Then he and his dog both drink a little water and the dog is given another opportunity to go potty. Finally, they head for ringside to await their turn. While waiting, Bond rubs down his dog's muscles to increase the dog's blood flow before going in the ring.

What about afterward? Do Bond and his dog slump into the nearest seats following their run? Not right away. Cooling down is every bit as important as warming up, so they take a leisurely walk, do a few stretches and the dog receives another rub down before they join their friends and relax at ringside.

Is it all necessary? "Yes," says Bond. "The saddest accident I've seen in the agility ring began when a handler came running up to the steward's table just as the class was about to conclude. She explained that she had become lost on the way to the trial and asked if she could still run her dog. Informed that she could, she quickly checked the course and dashed back to her truck to get her dog. Then she rushed her slightly overweight retriever out of the crate, had it jump to the ground (ouch!) and sprinted to the starting line without warming the dog up. Three jumps into the course, the retriever twisted into a turn for the next obstacle, yelped and stopped moving. It had torn a cruciate ligament. The injury could have been avoided if the dog had been in better condition and if the handler had allowed enough time for an adequate warm-up, or at least asked the judge for a few minutes to limber up prior to dashing into the ring.

"Remember, fatigue and physical stress are your biggest enemies in competition," says Bond. "A conditioned dog has greater reserves to combat fatigue and a limber, flexible dog can cope with the physical stresses of a challenging course."

LET BUTTERFLIES LINE-DANCE IN YOUR BELLY

You've memorized the course and warmed up, and novice competition is about to begin. Are you nervous? You bet you are. And believe it or not, it will work in your favor if you let it.

What makes your stomach do flip-flops, your hands sweat, your mouth go dry and sends you to the rest room every 15 minutes? A chemical called adrenaline. Adrenaline causes all that nervous energy when it's released into your blood stream, and every actor, athlete, musician or anyone else who cares about their performance contends with it. Some people love it. They find it stimulating and get hooked on the high. Other people dread it. They believe they can't think straight or control their muscles when they get that jittery feeling.

The truth is, nervous energy is natural. It's how our bodies react to a stressful or challenging situation. Adrenaline helped our cave man ancestors when flight or fight were the only choices by making them flee faster or fight harder than they could have without it. And it's still with us today. Whether you welcome it or not, adrenaline is ready to make you think clearer and move faster in the agility ring than you would without it. Sure it will put you on edge, but think of it as the competitive edge because adrenaline will help you perform better if you let it.

Letting your nervous energy help you is the hard part, because adrenaline creates an odd sensation that may make you uneasy at first. If you believe the butterflies in your belly have taken control of your brain and will make you lose your way on the course and forget your dog's name, you're not helping yourself at all. Instead, believe those butterflies are your body trying to help you, just as they helped your ancestors. Then, instead of letting them take control, teach them to dance to your tune.

Do you think you would do better if you could get rid of your nervous energy? It isn't true. Don't ever wish away your anxious feeling, because without a rush of adrenaline, you will lose your competitive edge. So how should you contend with precompetition flutters? The first step in taming your butterflies is to understand why you have them, and now you do. They're part of being human. Gaining experience is the second step. The more often you compete, the better you will learn to use, and even enjoy, your nervous energy. Even the agility stars who compete at the world championships have butterflies helping them think fast. The only difference between theirs and yours is they have tamed theirs just enough so they flutter in time to their favorite rhythm. With practice, yours will too.

IT'S YOUR TURN!

Before going in the ring, make sure you're in compliance with the regulations. Empty your pockets of treats and toys and take off or put on Beau's buckle collar if necessary, depending on which organization's rules govern the trial. Double tie your shoe laces and put a secure clip in your hair if it's threatening to fall in your face and block your view. Then give Beau whatever cue you use to get him jazzed for agility ("Go for it," "Wanna do agility?")—unless exciting him before his run makes him so exuberant that he misses contact zones and sails over the pause table. No one knows Beau better than you, so rev him up with play if he needs it, or keep him calm with long, gentle strokes if he's already wound too tight.

You will be told when it's okay to start (usually by the timekeeper) and Beau will be timed from the instant his nose crosses the starting line. If he's overly eager to be off and running, you may gently restrain him behind the line, but don't touch him after he starts. Stick to your plan as much as you can so you can help Beau connect with the contact zones and overcome the challenges. Keep one eye on him and the other on where you're going, and give your commands and signals early enough so he has time to react. Also, be sure to use the same signals and commands you always use with the same inflections in your voice that Beau is used to. Otherwise, he may lose concentration from fretting over what's wrong with you.

Because dogs are only dogs and handlers are only human, mistakes happen. Chapter 6 will tell you how to avoid the most common errors and what to do if they occur despite your best efforts. Also, review the circle correction under the heading "Correcting Mistakes" in Chapter 4. Most important, don't let your mistakes embarrass you. So what if you goofed in front of an audience? The agility exhibitors in the audience already know what it feels like to make mistakes in the ring. So do the judges. They are, or were, exhibitors too. That leaves the spectators. Did you ever watch a runner or cyclist flounder on a hill, but make it to the top in spite of the struggle? I bet you admired their effort, maybe even wished you had the determination or the courage to try such arduous exercise. Well, that's the way the spectators see you. You're out there doing a sport they can only watch. Maybe you're not the greatest agility handler, and Beau may lack a little finesse, but they admire you for training your dog and having the guts to go for it.

When Beau crosses the finish line, treat him as if he had the best run of his entire life even if you can't understand why he made so many mistakes. The truth is, he took a giant step just by performing in a strange place. Nothing is as important to your dog's agility career as his attitude toward competing. Making Beau feel good about it will build his confidence and eventually he'll work well in any competitive situation.

Don't be in a hurry to rush off after you finish your run. Stay and watch the other classes if possible, especially the advanced ones. Now that you know agility well enough to compete, it's incredible how much you will learn by watching the subtle handling techniques of the top handlers. While you are watching, don't forget your partner. Give him fresh water and an occasional treat, pet him and keep him happy and comfortable. If you're planning to spend hours at ringside, Beau may prefer a nice nap in his crate. Just make sure he's in the shade and gets plenty of air. Before leaving for home, offer him more water and take him on a nice walk.

APPRAISING BEAU'S PERFORMANCE

How is Beau doing in the agility ring? If you competed in more than five trials without earning a leg toward a novice title, try to remember what went wrong at each trial. Did Beau make different types of mistakes every time—sometimes missing a contact zone, other times refusing an obstacle or knocking the board off a jump—or did he make the same mistakes over and over?

If his mistakes varied from trial to trial, he simply isn't quite ready to compete yet. During practice, does he have an opportunity to try a variety of different sequences and does he almost always perform them well on the first try? If not, he needs more training. Discuss the problem with your instructor, if you have one. Otherwise, plan your practice sessions in advance by jotting down diagrams for a wide variety of sequences. Then enter your next trial after Beau has a high percentage of success with those sequences on his first try.

If he still makes mistakes in competition that never occur during practice, he's probably losing his concentration at the trial. There are several ways to cure this. One is to stay all day at the next trial, watching from a ringside seat with Beau beside you. When he relaxes enough to nap at ringside during an agility event, chances are he has become accustomed to the noise and activity and will be able to concentrate on the course next time. Another way to help Beau get over being stagestruck is to take along a tape recorder and record an hour of an agility event. Then play the tape at home when Beau is eating or while he naps.

If Beau completes most of each course but makes the same mistake at every trial, it's obvious what has to be corrected. Go all the way back to on-lead work and gradually take him through the steps of learning the obstacle or directional signal just as if he were never taught it before. When you are sure he understands it, set up several different sequences all containing Beau's old nemesis. When he gets it right every time, send in your next entry.

Unfortunately, it isn't always that easy. For example, if Beau always knocks down a jump or two, the problem could be something as simple as both of you going too fast, but chances are Beau needs serious help with jumping. Your instructor may be able to create jumps that will eventually improve his performance, and there are several excellent books available on teaching dogs how to jump properly. If Beau's jumping problems persist no matter what you or your instructor do, see your veterinarian. Beau may have a physical problem that makes it impossible for him to jump well.

Besides assessing Beau, assess yourself to make sure the way you handle under pressure isn't throwing off Beau's performance. Are you giving the same commands and signals you practiced in the same tone of voice—and are you giving them soon enough? Or are you trying something new and expecting Beau to read your mind? Ask a friend to give you an honest appraisal of your handling. Better yet, get someone to videotape your practice run at home and your run at the trial. Then compare them closely, looking for body language or mixed signals that could have confused Beau. It could be something as simple as your voice cracking or sounding squeaky from nerves. Correct it by becoming talkative just before your turn. Chat with a friend or talk to Beau right up to when the dog before you runs. Then take a moment to concentrate on your strategy and three deep breaths to help you relax. And have a good run.

YOU'RE HOOKED—NOW WHAT?

Maybe it was even more fun than you imagined. Or maybe it brought home the meaning of the slogan, "Do the thing you fear. Everything else is boring." For whatever reason, you want to attend more agility trials. Many more.

How often should you and Beau compete in agility? As often as you want, providing you are both enjoying yourselves and it isn't a financial drain on your family. Beau will let you know if you're overdoing it. Just watch his body language. If he used to spring across the start line and now he trots across it nonchalantly, he's losing his zest. He may need more creative and exciting practice sessions or more time off between trials.

Chances are you and Beau both love agility, but could use some expert help. It's coming right up. In the next chapter, top competitors, instructors and judges answer the questions novices ask most often and discuss the mistakes most frequently made at trials.

TRAINING TIPS
From the Pros

By now you've read enough about agility to know what type of obstacles you will encounter and what to expect at an event. That takes care of some "whats" but it doesn't deal with your "what ifs?" So I asked some popular agility judges and instructors to answer the questions their students most frequently ask, and to discuss the mistakes new handlers tend to make at trials and how to prevent them.

WHAT NEW STUDENTS WANT TO KNOW

How long will it take my dog to learn agility? This answer is from Stuart Mah, an agility instructor and judge from Jacksonville, Florida. Mah represented the USA at the World Agility Championships in 1995, 1996 and 1998.

When we teach agility, we aren't just teaching the dog to do things, we are teaching the handler to do things as well. Obstacle performance is only part of agility. Remember that agility is a team sport involving both handler and dog communicating and coordinating with each other to perform a course.

The best dog-handler teams in agility have a good working relationship. This relationship is not formed overnight. Like fine wine, it takes time to develop. Sometimes one team comes together more rapidly than another. It may take one dog-and-handler team only a few weeks to begin competing,

Agility judge, instructor and incredible competitor Stuart Mah sends Reese over an obstacle unique to international competition at the 1996 World Agility Championship in Switzerland.

while another team needs many months to get ready. This doesn't mean the slower developing team will not be as good as the faster developing team. It just means the dog and handler need more time to acquire the skills that will make them a good working partnership.

In addition, the process of learning to do agility is never ending. There is never a point where one can say, "My dog knows all about agility." There is always another, higher level that one can aspire to if they wish. To sum up, the dog and handler are always learning agility, from the time they start their first class until they retire from the sport.

Should I train both of my dogs at the same time? Stuart Mah has the answer again.

When beginning agility handlers train two dogs at the same time, the result is frequently two dogs that give mediocre performances at best. Each dog has different physical abilities, a different learning curve and a different amount of drive. Quite often a training technique that is right for one dog is not the best method for another dog. Yet novice agility trainers tend to forget that every dog is different and may try to train both dogs the same way, regardless of each dog's characteristics.

Also, new trainers have to learn the basic handling skills they need to compete well in the agility ring. When a new handler teaches two dogs at the same time, the handler and the dogs have a much harder time training and competing than they would if the handler gained experience with one dog before starting another.

In addition, in the heat of competition inexperienced handlers tend to forget which dog they are handling. This hinders, rather than helps, their partner. I would much rather see a person concentrate on one dog first, learn from that dog and allow the dog to become solid in agility. Once the handler has a firm grasp of the basic skills necessary for good handling, the second dog benefits from a more aware handler and almost always turns out better.

What should I do if I get lost on the course? S. Shane McConnell, an agility instructor and judge from Hinckley, Ohio, has the answer.

Look to see if the judge has signaled a wrong course penalty. If not, continue. If so, go back to the last correct obstacle your dog took in

S. Shane McConnell judges another agility judge, Lisa Layton and her dog Nitro. Nitro was the youngest dog to earn USDAA's Agility Dog Champion title and also set a USDAA record for the most qualifying scores in a row. Notice how he handles the contact zone.

sequence. Pick it up from whatever you can remember and go on as best you can. You may continue running the course, even if it's a wrong course, until you hear a whistle or cross the finish line.

May I ask to leave or be excused? I asked S. Shane McConnell.

Yes. If you feel you or your dog is injured, out of control, performing unacceptably or irretrievably lost on the course, you may ask to leave the ring. It is courteous to ask the judge's permission before exiting. No matter how awkward the situation, never behave in an unsportsmanlike manner.

What should I look for during the walk through? Again, I asked McConnell.

The first thing to look at is the course flow and sequence. Look at the locations of the start and finish lines. Next, assess the various challenge points around the course and establish your handling path. Also, you should always look at the course from your dog's point of view.

When can I enter my first trial? Agility instructors and judges Harry and Pat Guticz of Lincoln, Nebraska, answer this question.

Whenever you believe you and your dog are working together well as a team and can successfully complete a course. You should have already completed a variety of courses to your satisfaction many times in class.

What type (style) of agility is best? I asked Harry and Pat Guticz.

The one you are entered in next. All of the organizations provide fun and challenging courses. Each poses a different challenge and each should be appreciated for what it offers.

Do I have to purchase equipment so I can work my dog at home? Harry and Pat Guticz also answer this one.

No and yes. If you want to train at home (and you should), you can improvise. A hurdle can be anything your dog can safely leap over. For example, the cardboard tube from gift-wrap paper can be set on bricks, canisters or even across two chairs. An old sheet can become a closed tunnel. Ingenuity and duct tape can transform many everyday items into training aids. The one piece of equipment every agility competitor needs is weave poles (depending on the level you are striving for and the organization). Poles take the longest time to train and must be worked regularly using different numbers of poles to keep the dog working sharply.

Rocky can learn to take the tunnels just as well on this makeshift kids' tunnel as he can on a piece of professional agility equipment.

We can't make course time. How can I speed up my dog? I asked Mike Bond, an agility instructor and judge from Naperville, Illinois.

To correct this, I work with what motivates the dog. This may be certain foods, toys or balls. I start out working on the flat, no obstacles involved, teaching change of pace cues. "Hustle" and "Easy" are the ones I use. When the dog responds to "Hustle," I pay off with a reward. Each time, I expect slightly more speed than the time before until the appropriate speed is obtained. Once a standard is set, I will not reward anything less than our new standard.

When the concept is clear and the dog is consistently moving out with more drive and speed, I incorporate obstacles into the pace changes. First I make sure the dog fully understands and is comfortable on each obstacle. There have been numerous instances where the problem appeared to be lack of speed or desire, but wasn't. Instead, the dog responded slowly because he didn't know how to perform a particular obstacle.

Confusion will also slow dogs down. Make sure you are clear as to what you want your dog to do.

MISTAKES NOVICES MAKE MOST OFTEN AT TRIALS

Taking your eyes off your dog. Stuart Mah discusses this problem.

This is the single most common problem for new handlers. It can happen when you send your dog to perform an obstacle and then turn away, "breaking focus" with your dog. If you lose sight of your dog, however briefly, it can result in your dog running around the intended obstacle, or changing from one side of you to the other before you realize it. So don't assume that your dog will perform an obstacle just because you told him to.

Dogs are predators, and as such they are more keyed to motion than to sound. If a handler tells a dog "jump!," but turns away from the dog and the intended obstacle, the dog will move with the handler rather than take the jump. If a handler moves toward an obstacle and says nothing, but uses his eyes to keep the dog in his field of vision and "tracks" the dog to the intended obstacle, the dog can actually perform an obstacle (providing the dog has learned that obstacle) without the handler saying anything.

When practicing, it is important to keep your eyes on your dog. Work on this in class by watching your dog all the way into the intended obstacle, thus focusing the dog to the correct obstacle. As learning progresses, you can begin to focus the dog for longer periods of time and over more obstacles.

Harry and Pat Guticz of Lincoln, Nebraska also offer some advice on dealing with this problem.

Novice handlers often concentrate so much on the course (understandably not wanting to run the wrong course) that they forget to keep one eye on their dog at all times.

While walking the course, memorizing the pattern isn't enough. In addition, formalize a handling strategy so you know where you want to be to successfully guide and direct your dog through the course. You must also be mentally prepared to help your dog if he makes an error; in fact, you may have to collect, calm and redirect your dog.

Learning a course as discrete obstacles rather than as a sequence of obstacles. Stuart Mah discusses this mistake.

As a new handler, you may sometimes get lost on a course, even though the course appears to be fairly simple. This problem comes from learning a course as "obstacle 1—jump, obstacle 2—jump, obstacle 3—turn to a jump, obstacle 4—A-frame," and so on. What happens is that you are essentially memorizing each obstacle as a distinct course. So if there are a dozen obstacles on the course, and you run 12 courses of one obstacle each, you could certainly become confused and lose your way. The frequency with which a new handler gets lost increases with the number of obstacles in the course. Also, as the spacing of obstacles in a given area decreases, causing obstacle clutter, the potential increases for getting lost on the course.

One solution is to memorize the course as a sequence of shapes rather than individual obstacles. In the example above, rather than seeing four distinct obstacles, try to think of the sequence as "a three-jump turn to the A-frame," or "a J- or L-shaped sequence ending with the A-frame." By doing this, you will get a better feel for how the course is shaped and how it flows. It also decreases the amount you have to memorize. This becomes increasingly important in the advanced classes, where the courses are more complex.

Elizabeth never takes her eyes off Crackers as they work through the weave poles.

In addition, spend some time away from the ring mentally visualizing the sequences and then visualizing yourself running the course (seeing it in your mind's eye). Another way to help yourself remember courses is to actually run the course during the walk-through as if you were working your dog. This helps with the timing and visualization of the course. By the time you are ready to go into the ring, you will have already "run" the course one or more times, both physically and mentally.

Getting lost on the course. S. Shane McConnell talks about this common mistake.

Getting lost on the course is prevented primarily by learning to control your nerves, but there are also methods by which the course path can be memorized in small connecting segments. It is important for beginners to try to memorize the course by visualizing its flow; they should try not to read the numbers while they are running the course.

Showing before you are ready. This mistake, made by many, is discussed by Stuart Mah.

All too often a novice will enter an event to "see what happens." Frequently this results in the dog-handler team having problems, sometimes major ones, on the course. Sometimes the difficulties encountered on the course result in a training setback, or even a loss of confidence on the part of the handler or the dog.

To know if you are ready to show, ask yourself two questions. First, do I know the rules? A handler who doesn't know the rules by which agility is judged takes much for granted. I have seen handlers create problems on the course that resulted in significant fault penalties (including dismissal from the ring) because they didn't know the rules. Thus, before going into the agility ring know what you can and cannot do.

Second, ask yourself if your dog is ready. You should never have to "hope" that your dog will do something. For example, if you have to hope your dog will jump his required height, or if you have to hope your dog will perform a particular obstacle, you are better off not entering a trial. Wait until you are reasonably sure that your dog will perform any obstacle he might encounter at his level of competition (this differs among organizations—another reason to know the rules). Hoping your dog will do an obstacle puts undue mental or physical stress on both of you, and unprepared teams frequently fail. So be reasonably confident that your dog will do each obstacle before sending in your entry fees.

Not knowing the rules, including what is acceptable handling according to the organization whose trial you are attending. S. Shane McConnell addresses this.

The first step in learning the agility rules is to read a current rule book from each agility organization that interests you. Attending agility training classes is a valuable second step. It will help you understand how the rules are applied and interpreted. Finally, be attentive at trial briefings. The judge can clarify technical points and gray areas, and provides an opportunity to ask questions.

Overhandling, including bumping the dog. McConnell talks about this mistake that many beginners make.

Overhandling is usually the result of excessive nervousness or inadequate preparation. If in doubt, heed the advice of your instructor regarding your readiness to compete. Learn to trust your dog to execute the agility skills as he was taught. But remember, he can only do this if you handle with the same style and techniques you used in training.

Handling in a different manner than the dog is used to. Harry and Pat Guticz talk about this problem.

Under stress, novice handlers often run their dogs in a completely different manner than they do during training. They may get "frozen face syndrome" and move in a jerky, disjointed way. Also, the timing of the verbal and physical signals they give their dogs may be out of sync.

At the start line, calm yourself by taking three deep breaths. Then relax your muscles, give your dog a smile and handle him the same way and with the same tone of voice you used during practice.

Not working the contacts during the course familiarization. Harry and Pat Guticz explain why this is a mistake.

During course familiarization, handlers generally walk their dogs up to the obstacles and run them over the obstacles, but they don't "work the contacts." That means they handle these obstacles differently than they are to be performed. Don't confuse your dog this way. Instead, have him on lead during course familiarization, approach the obstacles at the speed you want during your run and "work" the contacts.

Jean Carter practices handling with Bandit on her right.

(*Note:* What is permitted during course familiarization differs among organizations—yet another reason to read the rules.)

Inability to handle the dog from the right side. This problem is discussed by agility judge Richard Budny of Greenfield, Wisconsin.

Handlers and dogs with an advanced obedience background sometimes have a hard time performing with the dog on the right-hand side. Consequently, simple side changes that are designed into the course become stumbling blocks. The handlers run around more obstacles than they have to and waste time doing it.

If you are an obedience handler, you will gain confidence working your dog off your right side through practice. Using right- and left-sided handling from the time you begin agility training will help.

Failing to warm up the dog before entering the ring. Richard Budny explains why this is a mistake.

During judging assignments, I often see handlers and dogs just standing around while waiting at ringside for their turn. Often the handler gets nervous or the dog gets excited just waiting around, and the result is a poor run. Instead of standing stiffly, massage your dog while waiting to go into the ring. It will loosen your dog's muscles and help calm your nerves. If you are running outdoors, throw a ball or Frisbee for your dog. He will love the play time and will be in a better mood for his run.

Giving up on your dog. Mike Bond talks about this ultimate mistake.

Novice handlers often give up on their dog right after a mistake is made. Their shoulders sag, their posture drops, their jaw sets on edge and they quit on their dog. From then on, they flip out their cues in a disgusted manner. When the team finishes, the dog retreats to the handler's stare or reprimand.

As a judge, I urge you not to quit on your partner. Keep agility upbeat. Keep it fun and challenging. Nine out of 10 mistakes are handler-induced anyway, and your dog doesn't quit on you. If you have a bad run, make a training session out of it (within the limits of the rules under which you are showing). You're a dance team. Some days you carry your partner and some days your partner carries you. No leg or title should be more important than your partner.

CHAPTER 7

WHAT'S *Next?*

It happened. You and Beau are both so turned on by agility, you want more events, bigger challenges and opportunities to work together in other ways. Here are some ideas on what you can strive for and how you can make the fun last forever.

HOW FAR CAN YOU GO?

How about Maribor, Slovenia? That's where the World Agility Championship were held in 1998. (They were held in Denmark in 1997 and Switzerland in '96, and will be in Dortmund, Germany in 1999). The American Kennel Club sent two agility teams to Slovenia: one for the Standard division (dogs 16 inches or taller) and one Mini team (dogs no taller than 15 3/4 inches). Each team has four dogs and handlers, plus an alternate.

Representing the USA at the World Agility Championship (a.k.a. the Agility Olympics) is the highest honor the sport offers, and only top dogs need apply. Candidates are judged on many factors, including winning major events and the ability to perform following a long airplane flight. To aid in team selection, the AKC has instituted an Intenational Sweepstakes Class. This non-regular class gives dog and handler teams the opportunity to demonstrate their abilities on a variety of international-style standard and jumpers courses. It is open only to dogs that are eligible to compete in both the Excellent Standard Class and the Excellent Jumpers With Weaves Class.

The USA team in Switzerland. In the front row are Karen Moureaux and Dallas, Nancy Gyes and Scud, Jane Simmons-Moake and Holly, Stuart Mah and Reece and Patti Hatfield and Lilly. Behind them, also in team colors, are Robert H. McKowen, the AKC vice president who made agility an AKC event, and Sharon Anderson, Field Director of AKC Agility and coach of the home team.

The American Kennel Club also holds an annual National Agility Championship in a different city every year. Dogs have to qualify to enter; the current requirements are four perfect scores at the standard Excellent level and two perfect scores at the Excellent Jumpers With Weaves level. The 1998 National Championship, held in Atlanta, Georgia, featured competition among 398 individual dogs as well as a state team tournament.

The USDAA's annual Grand Prix of Dog Agility, complete with banquets, entertainment and more than 20,000 spectators, is another one of our nation's most exciting agiity events. Dogs must qualify to enter, and regional qualifying events determine who gets to run at the prestigious Grand Prix. Locations and dates of qualifying events are announced in the *USDAA Dog Agility Report*.

ANIMAL-ASSISTED THERAPY

Beau doesn't have to qualify for national championship events to be an agility star. If he's well behaved and the happy-go-lucky type, he can attain superstar status just by performing an obstacle or two or obeying a couple of commands. Where will Beau's performance, or even his presence, always thrill the audience? At an institution for children, disabled people or senior citizens. It's a scientific fact that interacting with animals is therapeutic for people—and agility dogs, with their outgoing attitudes, make wonderful therapists.

All dogs, purebred or mixed, are welcome as animal-assisted therapy volunteers, and there are hundreds of therapy clubs across the nation. Requirements vary from one organization to another and sometimes from institution to institution, but generally Beau will have to pass one or more tests before being allowed to participate. The tests are to make sure he obeys simple commands, is manageable in strange places and pleasant to friendly strangers. Most agility dogs pass easily.

Beau's job as a therapy dog will vary with the institution. Sometimes there may be room to set up a few portable agility obstacles and perform for a crowd. Other times you and Beau will visit one patient at a time and Beau's

The AKC's agility world teams in Slovenia. In the front row, left to right, are Stuart Mah and Reece, Maggie Downey and Kelsey, Linda Mecklenburg and Nifty, Nancy Gyes and Scud, and Jerry Brown and Larrie. In the second row are AKC agility director Sharon Anderson, Marietta Huber and Squiggles, Katherine Leggett and Heather, Judy Keller and Morgan, Diane Bauman and Torville, and team coach Dan Dege. All the dogs have MX titles. The mini-team, made up of the dogs and handlers in the second row, took the gold medal.

job will be as simple as snuggling up to someone who needs a friend. Minor miracles have been attributed to therapy dogs. In Florida, a traumatized child smiled for the first time in months when a dog dropped a ball in his lap, and patients who remained mute for years have shocked their nurses by whispering their first hoarse words to a gentle dog.

While you and Beau might not make any miracles, there is always magic in animal-assisted therapy. Besides being good for the patients, it's also great for Beau. If he's still in his competitive years, meeting new people and interacting in strange settings will be good for his agility career. But when Beau is past his prime and retired from the agility ring, the benefits of being a therapy dog will be even greater. It's hard to go from superstar to has-been, but that never happens to a therapy dog. Beau will always be the focus of attention during his visits—forever talented, consistently a crowd-pleaser.

Are you a little nervous about your ability to interact with Beau's institutionalized audience? Just remember that Beau is the one giving the therapy. You are simply making it possible by sharing your dog with those who need him.

Want to find out more? Contact the organizations listed in the Appendix under "Animal-Assisted Therapy."

THE FRENZIED FUN OF FLYBALL

What's as much fun as agility and also has a following of screaming spectators? The game of flyball. Besides being a blast, it's convenient because it's often held in conjunction with an agility trial.

Flyball is a speedy relay race where two teams compete side by side on courses that are identical, with the possible exception of jump heights. Each team is made up of four dogs and four handlers. Flyball courses are straight, with four hurdles leading up to the flyball box at the far end. When the race begins, the first dog from each team is released, dashes over the hurdles and presses a lever on the box, making a tennis ball shoot out. The dog catches the ball and races back over the four hurdles. When he crosses the finish line, the next dog on the team is released. The team that finishes first, wins.

The North American Flyball Association (NAFA) presents flyball titles to dogs based on the number of points they accumulate. Points are awarded for especially speedy heats, so every dog on the team earns the same number of points for a fast time. Eight flyball titles are offered, beginning with Flyball Dog (FD) for earning 20 points and ending with the coveted Flyball Grand Champion title (FGRCh) for accumulating 30,000 points.

DOGS ARE FOR LOVING

Competitive spirit is a wonderful thing. It makes us learn things we might never have known, try things we might never have tried, go places we have never been before and strive to be even better than our best. But sometimes our competitive spirit grows so strong that it changes us. It can even make us forget what's really important and lure us into believing our happiness depends on the outcome of the next trial.

No matter how deeply involved in agility you become, always remember why you wanted a dog in the first place. Dogs are for companionship. Before any of us were competitors, we had dogs in our lives simply because we loved them.

Whenever competition is involved, moments of frustration alternate with times of elation. During the down days it may help to remember that before ribbons, trophies and agility titles, there was still a special relationship between dogs and people. Working together in the agility ring enhances that relationship, but frustration causes some trainers to tear it down—and that's a pity for both partners.

Please don't damage your dog's trust over a piece of colored ribbon or a couple of letters after his name. There's always another agility trial, but relationships are special.

When all is said and done, what's agility for? Fancee still thinks it's for fun. So does her owner, Bud Kramer.

Beau is welcome in flyball whether he is a purebred or not. Agility is a fine background for the sport because good jumpers and dogs that can concentrate on the game despite noisy arenas have a head start. Other prerequisites to success in flyball are a strong desire to retrieve and a special attachment to tennis balls. Of course, Beau has to be quick, alert, enthusiastic and in top physical condition to play a game as fast as flyball.

What if Beau has all the right attributes but he's just a little fellow? Would a flyball team want a tiny teammate? You bet they would. A small speed demon is a bonus to a flyball team because jump heights are set four inches lower than the shoulder height of the shortest dog on the team (the minimum height is eight inches and the maximum is 16 inches). That means one short dog will lower the jumps for the whole team. Naturally, many teams are glad to have at least one small but competitive member.

For more information, write to the "Flyball" addresses in Appendix A.

AS YOUR DOG AGES

One day Beau will be a little too old for agility competition. You'll know it because he'll consistently finish with slower times or he'll be stiff the day after a trial. While his body may stop him from being competitive, his spirit will soon miss the spotlight. Of course you won't want to quit your sport, so chances are you'll start training a young dog for the agility ring. If so, make Beau the youngster's mentor. While Beau demonstrates an obstacle and soaks up the praise he has learned to love, the young dog will learn by watching and become eager to try it, too.

When you take your young dog to agility class, bring Beau along if it's okay with the instructor. The old boy could be a demo dog for beginner classes, influencing the novice dogs as he works the obstacles with joy, enthusiasm and control. Best of all, the light work will keep Beau's body fit and his mind sharp, and he'll get to spend many hours at his favorite place—an agility course.

Organizations and Clubs

GENERAL OR MULTI-ACTIVITY ORGANIZATIONS OFFERING AGILITY

American Kennel Club (AKC)
5580 Centerview Dr., Suite 200
Raleigh, NC 27606
(919) 233-9767
Fax: (919) 233-3627
e-mail: INFO@akc.org
www.akc.org

United Kennel Club (UKC)
100 East Kilgore Rd.
Kalamazoo, MI 49001
(616) 343-9020
Fax: (616)343-7037
www.ukcdogs.com

American Mixed Breed Obedience Registry (AMBOR)
205 1st St. S.W.
New Prague, MN 56071
(612) 758-4598

National 4-H Council
7100 Connecticut Ave.
Chevy Chase, MD 20815-4999
Some 4-H clubs offer agility. To
find your local 4-H club, call your
state Extension Service, listed under
"County Government Offices" in
the phone book.

NATIONAL AGILITY ORGANIZATIONS

United States Dog Agility Association (USDAA)
P.O. Box 850955
Richardson, TX 75085-0955
(214) 231-9700
Fax: (214) 503-0161
e-mail: info@usdaa.com
www.usdaa.com

North American Dog Agility Council (NADAC)
HCR 2, Box 277
St. Maries, ID 83861
(208) 689-3803
www.teleport.com/~jhaglund/nadachom.htm

Australian Shepherd Club of America (ASCA)
6091 East State Highway 21
Byran, TX 77803-9652
(409) 778-1082
e-mail: asca@mail.myriad.net

Agility Association of Canada (AAC)
638 Wonderland Road South
London, Ontario, Canada N6K 1L8
(519) 473-3410

LOCAL AGILITY CLUBS

This is a partial list, as there are more clubs forming all the time.

Alabama

Magic City Canine Club
Carol C. Burt
504 St. Annes Cr.
Birmingham, AL 35244
(205) 991-3135
e-mail: cburt@2ab.com

North Alabama Canine Cruisers
Susan Hawkins
1050 Dockside Dr. #807
Huntsville, AL 35824
(256) 464-5353
e-mail: hawkinss@nichols.com

Alaska

Alaska Australian Shepherd Club
Joyce Angell
P.O. Box 212052
Anchorage, AK 99521-2052

Artic Streakers Agility Club
Kay Kirkland
8100 Clear Haven Circle
Anchorage, AK 99507

Arizona

Contact Zonies
Pat Stauber
8725 Edward Ave.
Scottsdale, AZ 85250
(602) 948-9002

Good Dog Agility Club
Jennifer Meyer
1080 E. Flint St.
Chandler, AZ 85225
(602) 899-8047

Jumping Chollas Agility Club
Billie Rosen
5301 W. Monte Cristo Ave.
Glendale, AZ 85306

Saguaro Scramblers Agility Club, Inc.
Maureen Odenwald
3007 E. Seneca St.
Tucson, AZ 85716-3024
(520) 323-6689

California

Agility Club of San Diego, Inc.
Robyn Broock
6734 Rockglen Ave.
San Diego, CA 92111
(619) 277-4793

Canine Agility Team
Ann Huie & Iris Berry
c/o 405 1st St.
Clovis, CA 93612

Contact Point Agility
Karen Moureaux
6952 Semrad Rd.
West Hills, CA 91307

County Wide Dog Training Club
Debbie Stoner
499 Pleasant Hill Rd.
Sebastopol, CA 95472

Dog Agility Racing Team
Barbara Mah
3971 Boyer
Chino, CA 91710
(909) 590-1170

Fresno Canine Agility Team
Ann Huie
405 First St.
Clovis, CA 93612
(209) 299-8724

Haute Dawgs Agility Group
Donna D. Amico
1328 Fitch Way
Sacramento, CA 95864
(916) 483-3294

Northern California Agility and Obedience Club
Virginia Isaac
5882 Woodleigh Dr.
Carmichael, CA 95608

Nothin' But Agility
Pamela Richards
36 Vineyard Ave.
San Anselmo, CA 94960

**Redwood Empire Australian
Shepherd Club**
Bruce Vincent
12551 Peach Lane
Wilton, CA 95693

Santa Barbara Flyers
Bruce Brackman
P.O. Box 3391
Santa Barbara CA 93105
(805) 549-5674

Seaside Scramblers Agility Center
Nancy Soyster
1830 Harvest Ln.
Camarillo, CA 93012
(805) 529-4452

The Bay Team
Nancy Gyes
10711 Crothers Rd.
San Jose, CA 95127
(408) 729-6942

West Valley Dog Sports
Sharon Kihara
1845 Purdue Ave. #1
Los Angeles, CA 90023
(310) 478-2885

Colorado
All Colorado Agility Team
Kent Mahan
4 Sandcastle Ct.
Pueblo, CO 81001
(719) 545-8461
e-mail: mahan@aculink.net

Front Range Agility Team
Cindi Macklin
30217 Sunset Trail
Pine, CO 80470
(303) 838-3434

Rocky Mountain Agility Team
Zona Tooke
8901 W. 51st Ave.
Arvada, CO 80002
(303) 456-7400
e-mail: Rmagility @aol.com

**Southern Colorado Australian
Shepherd Club**
Kent Mahan
4 Sandcastle Ct.
Pueblo, CO 81001

Twin Peaks Dog Club, Inc.
Susan Kurzweil
4765 West County Rd. 14
Loveland, CO 80537

Florida
Canopy Roads Crew
J.A. Lammert
84 Finner Dr.
Crawfordville, FL 32327

**Dog-On-It Agility Club of Or-
lando**
Joan Harrison
1105 Gator Lane
Winter Springs, FL 32708
(407) 699-0328

Gold Coast United Dog Club
B. Bailey
5785 SW 160th Ave.
Ft. Lauderdale, FL 33331
(945) 434-6344

Marion-Alachua Dog Training Association, Inc.
Laureen Ford
12009 NE 8th Ct.
Ocala, FL 34479
(352) 629-1427

Pals & Paws, Inc.
Cheryl Koehler
12094 Staggerbush Ct.
Jacksonville, FL 32223
(904) 262-3653

Tailwaggers Learning Center
Rachel Flatley
7135 Pigeon Key Way
Lake Worth, FL 33467
(407) 966-1367

United Bay Area Dog Obedience Group
L. R. Snelling
6241 60th Ave. N.
St. Petersburg, FL 33709
(813) 545-5764

United Dog Training Club of St. Petersburg
Lorrie Reed
4365 66th Ave. N.
Pinellas Park, FL 34665
(813) 528-2103

United IPOC
B. Craig
3236 Cullman Dr.
Lakeland, FL 33805

United Ketch
K.P. Carter
6933 Orient Rd.
Tampa, FL 33610
(941) 687-1881

Wag 'n' Train Agility Group
Joni Ress
6017 Woodale, Dr.
Lakeland, FL 33811
(941) 646-4986
e-mail: tachae@aol.com

Georgia

Canine Capers
Chris Danielly
6006 Fruithurst Lane
Norcross, GA 30092
(770) 448-5204
e-mail: cdanielly@aol.com

Sirius Dog Agility Training Center
4725 Old Highgate Entry
Stone Mountain, GA 30083
(404) 294-4359
e-mail: meryl@gsu.edu

Idaho

St. Maries Agility for Canines Club
Sharon Nelson
HCR 2 Box 277
St. Maries, ID 83861

Illinois

Agility Ability Club of Illinois
Dr. Mike Bond
232 Creed Rd.
Plano, IL 60545
(630) 552-9007

Blitzen Canine Academy, Inc.
Pamela Juliano
17625 S. Ridgeland
Tinley Park, IL 60477
(708) 532-0939

Burr Ridge Dog Training Center
G. Gregorich
606 Valley Dr.
LeMont, IL 60439
(630) 257-2767

Creekwood Meadows Agility Club
Cherie Bond
232 Creed Rd.
Plano, IL 60545
(630) 552-9007

Four Paws Training Club
Nancy Foster
1080 White Rd.
Antioch, IL 60002
(847) 838-0322

Kickapoo Kreek K9 Klub
Debbie Kumpe
1527 Hendryx Pl.
Peoria, IL 61615
(309) 692-7328

LBJ&M Dog Training and Agility Club
Jan Casella
6955 Sweard
Niles, IL 60714

Northern Illinois Bouvier Des Flanders Club
N. Eilks
5689 Hwy. S
Lake Mills, WI 53551
(920) 648-3192

On Course Agility
Karen Holik
3N735 Kenwood
West Chicago, IL 60185
(708) 687-5289

Paws 4 Fun
Gail Storm
10121 N. Henderson Rd.
Orangeville, IL 61060
(815) 789-3141

Simon Sez Agility, Inc.
Karen and Frank Holik
476 N. Fairfield
Lombard, IL 60148

Smack-Dab's Obedience Training, Inc.
Kathy Fay
1559 Abbotsford Dr.
Naperville, IL 60563
(630) 357-9549

Windy City Agility Club
Joan Witas-Marec
6641 Forestview Dr.
Oak Forest, IL 60452
(708) 687-5289

Indiana
E.C.H.O. Club, Inc.
G. Hay
57269 Poppy Rd.
South Bend, IN 46619-9417
(219) 287-0218

Elkhart County Humane Obedi-ence Club, Inc.
Kris Goodenough
4403 Spring Creek Rd.
Galien, MI 49113

Paw Power Blues Dog Club
A Kaszak
119 E. 141st St.
Riverdale, IL 60827
(708) 841-6035

Trail Creek Dog Training Club, Inc.
Joe Reese
P.O. Box 8622
Michigan City, IN 46360
(219) 326-8426

IOWA
Fort Dodge Canine Companion Club
Pat Saunders
1019 S. 24th St.
Ft. Dodge, IA 50501
(515) 576-6460

4RK9's Inc.
Susan Hansen
5841 Shiloh Lane NE
Cedar Rapids, IA 52411
(319) 393-0112

Kansas
Agility Ability of Greater Kansas City
Kim Anderson
1-232 Switzer
Overland Park, KS 66212

Dodge City Kennel Club
S. Clinesmith
503 Sierra Ct.
Dodge City, KS 67801
(316) 227-5404

Heartland Dog Training Club
Cheryl May
2005 Somerset Square
Manhattan, KS 66503
e-Mail: UD@nasw.org

Hutchinson Kennel Club, Inc.
E. Cheely
4706 Scott Lane
Hutchinson, KS 67502
(316) 662-7453

The United Lawrence Jayhawk Kennel Club
Vickie Jacobs
7045 SW 61st St.
Tecumseh, KS 66542
(785) 379-5430

Triune Canine Training Club
Joan Oberhelman
8410 Edgerton Rd.
De Soto, KS 66018
(913) 583-1747

Kentucky
Derby City Agility Association
Pat Kerschner
235 Alpha Ave.
Louisville, KY 40218

Louisiana
Pawprints Agility Club
Patt Elmore
2918 Hoyte
Shreveport, LA 71118
(318) 686-9429

Maine
Promised Land Agility Club
Kim Tees
P.O. Box 388
Raymond, ME 04071
(207) 655-2122

Maryland
Artful Dodgers Agility Group
Janet Gauntt
10489 State Road 108
Columbia, MD 21044
(410) 715-9923

Kinder-Pup, Inc.
Terry Wright
60 D Johnson Rd.
Pasadena, MD 21122

Maplefield Agility
Nancy Williams
2507 Fairmount Rd.
Hampstead, MD 21074
(410) 374-1556

Massachusetts
ACE Agility Club
Dave Nitka
589 North St.
Feeding Hills, MA 01030-1309
(413) 786-5344
e-mail: kaneonapua@Yahoo.com

Act-Up Agility Club
Alanna Kelly
197 Vernon St.
Norwood, MA 02062

ARFF Agility Club, Inc.
Sandy Cody
26 Hilltop Dr.
Bedford, MA 01730
(781) 275-1964

Pioneer Valley Kennel Club
Doris Viguers
43 Eden Trail
Bernardston, MA 01337

Michigan

Agility Workout Society of Mid-Michigan
Joe Sare
899 Keith Ave.
Oxford, MI 48371
(248) 628-6366
joe_Sare@MSN.com

Canine Combustion Agility Group
Lesley O'Neil
27600 Larchmont
St. Clair Shores, MI 48081
(810) 775-6452

Capital City Canine Club
Elaine Striler
7010 E. Grand River
Laingsburg, MI 48848
(517) 651-6695

Cherrybrook Agility
Wynell Brush
8110 W. Eaton Hwy.
Grand Ledge, MI 48837
(517) 627-9452

Dogsports of Genese County
P. Ash
5362 Hopkins
Flint, MI 48506
(810) 736-8918

Grand Rapids Agility Club, Inc.
Ellen Hizer
1317 Houseman NE
Grand Rapids, MI 49505

Muskegon Lakeshore Obedience Training Club
Clarence Degraves
2200 Shettler Rd.
Muskegon, MI 49444
(616) 733-0987

White River Dog Training Group, Inc.
S. Henry
14162 N. Beech
Reed City, MI 49677

Minnesota

A-1 Dog Training Center
Jan Frey
11824 Mississippi Dr.
Champlin, MN 55316

Arrowhead Agility Club
Diane Herald-Craig
5154 N. Tischer Rd.
Duluth, MN 55804
(218) 525-3973

Canine Agility Center of Central Minnesota
Earl Kyle
114 N. 33rd Ave.
St. Cloud, MN 56303
(320) 251-7814
e-mail: EarlKYLE@cloudnet.com

Minnesota Agility Club
Renee Ward
6300 Morgan Ave. S.
Richfield, MN 55423
(612) 866-8866

Mississippi
Bark, Inc.
Susan Burton
P.O. Box 903
Brandon, MS 39043
(601) 824-0202
e-mail: toothdoc@netdoor.com

Missouri
Agility Ability of Greater Kansas City, Inc.
J. Orr
5405 W. Gale Cr.
Smithville, MO 64089
(816) 532-4898

Greater St. Louis Agility Training Club
Stephanie Ritter
632 Village Square Dr.
Hazelwood, MO 63042

Moberly Missouri Kennel Club, Inc.
Michael Moore
Rt. 1 Box 160B
Holliday, MO 65285

Springfield Missouri Dog Training Club, Inc.
V. Steever
4225 FM RD 488
Marshfield, MO 65706
(417) 859-4903

Nebraska
Go Dogs! Inc.
Greg Ruhe
2338 No 83rd St.
Omaha, NE 68134
(402) 334-7941

Greater Lincoln Obedience Club, Inc.
Robert Miller
P.O. Box 57333
Lincoln, NE 68505
(402) 467-2835

Star City Agility Team
Pat Guticz
2785 E Street
Lincoln, NE 68510
(402) 435-7255

Nevada
Great Western Rottweilers
Priscilla Phillips
13025 Broili Dr.
Reno, NV 89511
(702) 851-3637

New Jersey

Bayshore Companion Dog Club, Inc.
Victoria Brown
197 Dey Grove Rd.
Englishtown, NJ 07726
(732) 446-3219

New Mexico

Southwest Agility Team
Corlyn Burkett
913 Lomas Ct. NE
Albuquerque, NM 87112
(505) 296-4849
e-mail: SABACOR@AOL.com

North Carolina

Autumn Winds Agility Club
Donald Stogner
102 McDole Circle
Cary, NC 27511
(919) 362-5909

Blue Ridge Agility Club
Maureen Robinson
200 Old Zirconia Rd.
Zirconia, NC 28790

Bon-Clyde Agility
Bonnie Buchanan
P.O. Box 2208
Sanford, NC 27331-2208

New Hampshire

All Dogs Gym Agility
Gail Fisher
801 Perimeter Rd.
Manchester, NH 03103
(603) 669-4644

Canine Agility Training Society
Mark Wirant
29 Blossom St.
Keene, NH 03431
(603) 352-7276

New England Agility Team
Mark Stone
P.O. Box 73
Salem, NH 03079-0073
e-mail: SunnySkye@Juno.com

New Jersey

Skyline Agility Club
Christine Miele
147 Central Ave.
Old Tappan, NJ 07675

New York

Contact Agility Group
Claudia Mohr
55 Rymph Rd.
Lagrangeville, NY 10605
(914) 223-7963

Fun Agility Sports Team
Grian Young
44 Green Ave.
Castleton, NY 12033
(518) 732-2180

Long Island Agility
Arthur Weiss
11 Keeler St.
Huntington, NY 11743
(516) 427-5672

Ohio
Buckeye Region Agility Group
Pam Williams
1379 Goldmill Way
Columbus, OH 43204
(614) 351-0242
e-mail: GOOSIELU@infinet.com

Columbus Agility
Susan Thomas
5159 Northcliff Loop E
Columbus, OH 43229

Erie Shores Dog Training Club
B. Laity
6006 Vandalia
Brooklyn, OH 44144
(330) 894-1143

Gem City Dog Club
Ron Schumann
2153 Crab Tree Dr.
Beavercreek, OH 45431-3311
(513) 426-9528

Medina Swarm
Dr. Shane McConnell
P.O. Box 344
Sharon Center, OH 44274
(330) 239-0603

Northwest Ohio Dog Trainers
Pete and Sal Mansell
Rt. 2 03501 - Q
Edon, OH 43518

Performance Agility Working Society of Ohio
Tammi Skillman
7070 Lighthouse Pt.
Maineville, OH 45039

Toledo Timebusters
Pete Mansell
03501 County Road Q
Edon, OH 43518
(419) 459-4836

Oklahoma
OKPaws Agility Club
S. Adams
3012 NW 32nd St.
Oklahoma City, OK 73112
(405) 946-6491

Tulsa Agility Club, Inc.
Richard Beeby
2206 S 83 E Ave.
Tulsa, OK 74129
(918) 663-9250

Oregon
Columbia Agility Team
H. Gercke
19363 Willamette Dr. #245
West Linn, OR 97068

Willamette Agility Group
Erin Cimbri
2882 N.E. Sherwood Place
Corvallis, OR 97330
(541) 758-0254

Pennsylvania
Flexible Flyers Agility Group
Barbara DeMascio
2 Wren Rd.
Gilbertsville, PA 19525
(610) 367-9239

Keystone Agility Club
Ardis Lukens
508 New Elm St.
Conshohocken, PA 19428
(610) 825-7491

South Carolina
Carolina Obedience and Agility Trainers
Karen Orr
478 Pistol Club Rd.
Easley, SC 29640

Low Country Dog Agility
Margaret Connell
P.O. Box 895
Mt. Pleasant, SC 29465
(803) 881-3038

Texas
Bexar Regional Agility Team
Rosalie Hauser
7463 Branston
San Antonio, TX 78250
(210) 520-7527

Dallas Agility Working Group
Pat Horton
909 Creek Valley
Mesquite, TX 75181
(972) 222-3136

Dallas Dog Sports
Patty Drom
2760 Pecan Dr.
Wylie, TX 75098
(972) 442-9226

Houston Ruff 'N Ready Dog Agility
Joanne Lutterman
505 N. Post Oak Lane
Houston, TX 77024
(713) 682-4528

Leaps and Bounds Agility Center
Elizabeth Blanchard
8135 Bo Jack Dr.
Houston, TX 77040
(713) 744-6215

New Hope Agility Group
Donna Arnold
P.O. Box 387
Columbus, TX 78934

Panola Agility Canine Klub
Ann Bridges
139 Lake Park Rd.
Carthage, TX 75633
(903) 693-4888

RUK-9 Agility Group
Annette Napoli
3307 Sam Houston Dr.
Sugarland, TX 77479
(281) 980-6342

The Good Dog Positive Obedience Training & Agility Club of Fort Worth
Claudia Iannaci
7708 Incline Terrace
Fort Worth, TX 76179

Travis Agility Group
Gloria Wilson
4202 Tamarack Tr.
Austin, TX 78729-2850
(512) 255-5661

Vermont
Canine Agility Training Society
Lou Wittmer
P.O. Box 42
Vernon, VT 05354

Virginia
Belroi Agility Club
Nelson Fletcher
6023 Gallopond Lane
Gloucester, VA 23061
(804) 693-2167

Chesapeake Bay Achievers
Sherry Bryant
4015 Oak Dr.
Chesapeake, VA 23321
(757) 484-4516

Dog Owners Training Club of Lynchburg, Inc.
Clair Malinowski
102 Walnut Place
Lynchburg, VA 24502
(804) 237-1916

Mattaponi Kennel Club, Inc.
L. Kauffman
10190 Bens Way
Manassas, VA 20110
(703) 368-1373

Tidewater Dog Performance Club
D. Bright
1044 W. Oceanview Ave.
Norfolk, VA 23503
(757) 480-9621
e-mail P. Wilson:
AgileDog@juno.com

Touch & Go Agility Club
Sue Weis
1907 Wilson Lane
McLean, VA 22102
(703) 442-0445

Washington
Chuckanut Chaotic Canines
Ellen Kreider
4720 - 268th NW
Stanwood, WA 98292

Rainier Agility Team
Sandra Katzen
3016 22nd Ave. S
Seattle, WA 98144
(206) 725-2718

Spokane Dog Training Club
Barb Benner
15407 W. Teepee
Spokane, WA 99224
(509) 244-2332

Wisconsin
Fun On the Run Agility Group
Stacy Peardot
6896 Hwy KW
Belgium, WI 53004
(414) 285-7098

Milwaukee Dog Training Club
Joan Mullen
W186-N, 7064 Marcy Rd.
Menomonee Falls, WI 53051
(414) 253-6789

Sta-Lyn K-9 Training Center
Jeanine Daugherty
2068 S. 55th St.
West Allis, WI 53219

CANADIAN AGILITY CLUBS

This is a partial list as more clubs are forming all the time.

Alberta
Alberta Junior Kennel Club
P.O. Box 43054
Calgary, AB
Canada T2J 7A7

Calgary Agility Association
Gro Aasgaard
3136 - 46 Street SW
Calgary, AB
Canada T3E 3W8

Calgary Cruizin' Canines Agility Club
Michelle Ooms
59 Cedardale Mews SW
Calgary, AB
Canada T2W-5G4
(403) 238-3762

Lloydminster Kennel and Obedience Club
Carol Bevan
5632 - 39 St.
Lloydminster, AB
Canada T9V 1K2

Northland Kennel Club
Box 5799
Fort McMurray, AB
Canada T9H 3G5

British Columbia
Capital Comets
Shelly Welsh
2021 Goodridge Sooke, BC
Canada V0S 1N0

Coast Canines
Sue Spurgeon
P.O. Box 1342
Sechelt, BC
Canada V0N 3A0
e-mail: s spurgeon@sunshine.net

Cowichan Obedience Club
Mary Young
1125 Briarwood Circle, RR#1
Cobble Hill, BC
Canada V0R 1L0

Dogwood Pacesetters Canine Sports Club
Maren Middleton
13513 88 Ave.
Surry, BC
Canada V3V 1A1
e-mail: rick palylyk@mindlink.ca

Dog Star Canine Sports
Wesley Barnaby
17977-64th Ave.
Coverdale, BC
Canada V3S 1Z3
e-mail: barnabyw@citywidenet.com

Jump Start Dog Agility Training
Dee Gleed
24202 56th Ave.
Langley, BC
Canada V2Z 2N9

K-9 Cliffhangers Canine Sports Club
Peter Savage
1562 Bond St., BC
Canada V7J 1EJ

North Okanagan Lightening Bolts
Barbara Anderson
Site 1, Com 79, RR#7
Vernon, BC
Canada V1T 7Z3

Paws Agility
Mardi Douglass
1925 Brighton Ave.
Victoria, BC
Canada V8S 2C7

Pooch Palace
RR#1, Box 24
Sales Site
Quesnel, BC
Canada V2J 3H5

Sooke All Breed Obedience Club
P.O. Box 1293
Sooke, BC
Canada V0S 1N0

Viewpoint Dog Training
Karen Palylyk
33678 Elizabeth Ave.
Abbotsford, BC
Canada V4X 1T4
e-mail: rick palylyk@mindlink.bc

Manitoba

Agility in Manitoba
Gisele Savard Marion
132 Genthon St.
Winnipeg, MB
Canada R2H 2J5

New Brunswick

Flyball Agility Maritime Express
Gwen Dingee
RR #8
Moncton, New Brunswick
Canada E1C 8K2

Newfoundland

Companion Dog Trainers Ltd.
728 Main Road, Box 84
Goulds, Newfoundland
Canada A1S 1G3

Nova Scotia

Bluenose Agility & Recreational Canines
July Langille
62 Scotia St.
Bridgewater, Nova Scotia
Canada B4V 1E8

Canine Agility Assoc. of Nova Scotia
Carolyn Dockrill
89 Etter Rd.
RR 2
Mount Uniacke, Nova Scotia
Canada B0N 1Z0
Web Site: http://is.dal.ca/
~mowbray/agility/index.htm

Ontario

All Dog Sports Club
Art Newman
RR #3
North Gower, Ontario
Canada K0A 2T0

Champlain Dog Club
G. Charette
905 Pembroke St. E
Pembroke, Ontario
Canada K8A 3M3

Flyin' Fidos Dog Agility Club
Kim Cooper
80 De Long
Gloucester, Ontario
Canada K1J 7E1

Hilltop K9 Agility
RR#1
Summertown, Ontario
Canada K0C 2E0

K-9 Sports Park Ltd.
Anette Hogel
5327 Britannia Rd. RR #6
Milton, Ontario
Canada L9T 2Y1

K-9 Studio Agility Dog Association
575 N. Court St.
Thunder Bay, Ontario
Canada P7A 4Y5

Middlesex Agility Club
Dorinda Desmet
1342 Alersbrook Rd.
London, Ontario
Canada N6G 3J3

Power Paws Canine Agility Group
Roberta Malott
Box 908
Blenheim, Ontario
Canada N0P 1A0

Swansea Dog Obedience Club
Carol Mayeda
6 Glenroy Ave.
Etobicoke, Ontario
Canada M8Y 2M1

Tamsu Learning Centre
John Mairs
RR #4
Tottenham, Ontario
Canada L0G 1W0

Temiskaming Kennel Club
Shirley Bond
Box 639
Lew Liskeard, Ontario
Canada P0J 1P0

Quebec

Agilite Canine Centre
Mauricie Eric Laliberte
1600 - 50 Avenue
Grand-Mere, Quebec
Canada G9T 6N6

Club Agilite Canin De St. Lazare
Irene Krebs
1599 Blueberry Hill
St. Lazare, Quebec
Canada J0P 1V0

Club Agilite Rive Sud
Roger Pierre
Cote 12 Valois
St. Constant, Quebec
Canada J5A 1P5

Club d'agilite de la Monteregie
M. J. Thuot
990 Colborne
Chambly, Quebec
Canada J3L 3E4
e-mail: agile.tila@sympatico.co

Club D'Agilite Des Ruisseaux
Claire Latour
222 Boischatel
Pt. Viau Laval, Quebec
Canada H7G 1J2

L A-Dresse Canine, Inc.
255 Av St. Sacrement St.
Sacrement, Quebec
Canada G1N 3X8

Saskatchewan
PADOC K9's and Kompany
Kim Plummer
RR#5, Site 32, Box 23
Prince Albert, Saskatchewan
Canada S6V 5R3

Prairie PDQ Dogsports
Elsie Wesdyk
Box 93
Pense, Saskatchewan
Canada S0G 3W0

Saskatchewan Agility Association
1414 McKercher Dr.
Saskatoon, Saskatchewan
Canada S7H 5A8

Wonderdogs Agility Gang of Saskatoon
Site 500, Box 4
RR 5
Saskatoon, Saskatchewan
Canada S7K 3J8

AGILITY IN PUERTO RICO

Puerto Rico Dog Agility Association, Inc.
Abel DeVarona
MSC 676 Winston Churchill Ave.
138
San Juan PR 00926-6023

FOR INFO ON OBEDIENCE
Contact AKC, UKC or AMBOR (above)

FLYBALL

North American Flyball Association
P.O. Box 8
Mt. Hope, Ontario
Canada LOR 1W0

ANIMAL-ASSISTED THERAPY

Delta Society
Pet Partners Program
P.O. Box 1080
Renton, WA 98057
(206) 226-7357

Therapy Dogs International
6 Hilltop Rd.
Mendham, NJ 07945
(908) 429-0670

Therapy Dogs Incorporated
P.O. Box 2786
Cheyenne, WY 82003
(307) 638-3223

Recommended Reading

GENERAL INTEREST

Books

The Complete Dog Book, 19ᵗʰ Edition Revised, by the American Kennel Club. New York: Howell Book House, 1998.

Magazines and Newsletters

AKC Gazette (and *Events Calendar*), American Kennel Club. Subscription information: (919) 233-9780.

AMBOR Highlights, The American Mixed Breed Obedience Registration, 205 1st St. SW, New Prague, MN 56071; (612) 758-4598.

Bloodlines, United Kennel Club, 100 E. Kilgore Rd., Kalamazoo, MI 49001-5597; (616) 343-9020.

AGILITY

Books

Agility Training, the Fun Sport for All Dogs, by Jane Simmons-Moake. New York: Howell Book House, 1991.

The Clothier Natural Jumping Method, by Suzanne Clothier. Flying Dog Press, P.O. Box 290AB, Stanton, NJ 08885; (800) 7-FLY-DOG.

Jumping From A to Z: Teaching Your Dog to Soar, by M. Chris Zink, D.V.M., Ph.D., and Julie Daniels. Canine Sports Productions, 1810A York Rd., #360, Lutherville, MD 21093.

Peak Performance, Coaching the Canine Athelete, by M. Chris Zink, D.V.M., Ph.D. Canine Sports Productions, 1810A York Rd., #360, Lutherville, MD 21093.

Rules and Regulations

North American Dog Agility Council Rule Book, NADAC, HCR 2, Box 277, St. Maries, ID 83861.

Official Rules & Regulations of the United States Dog Agility Association, Inc., USDAA, P.O. Box 850955, Richardson, TX 75085-0955.

Regulations for Agility Trials, single copy available free from the American Kennel Club, 5580 Centerview Dr., Suite 200, Raleigh, NC 27606-3390; (919) 233-9780.

Rules, Special Edition, United Kennel Club, 100 E. Kilgore Rd., Kalamazoo, MI, 49001-5597; (616) 343-9020.

Magazines and Newsletters

The Contact Line, Cascade Publications, 401 Bluemont Circle, Manhattan, KS, 66502-4531; (913) 537-7022.

USDAA Dog Agility Report, P.O. Box 850955, Richardson, TX 75085-0955.

The Clean Run, Bud Houston and Monica Percival, 35 Walnut St., Turner Falls, MA 01376; (413) 863-8308, E-mail: cleanrun@msn.com.

The Magazine for Dog Agility, P.O. Box 2851, Santa Clara, CA 95055-2851; E-mail: AgilityMag@aol.com.

OBEDIENCE

Obedience Regulations, single copy available free from the American Kennel Club, 5580 Centerview Dr., Suite 200, Raleigh, NC 27606-3390.

DOG SHOWING

A Beginner's Guide to Dog Shows, single copy available free from the American Kennel Club, 5580 Centerview Dr., Suite 200, Raleigh, NC 27606-3390.

FLYBALL

The Finish Line Magazine, 4365 Glancaster Rd., Mt. Hope, Ontario, Canada LOR 1W0.

Flyball Racing, by Lonnie Olson. New York: Howell Book House, 1997.

THERAPY

Volunteering With Your Pet, by Mary Burch, Ph.D. New York: Howell Book House, 1996.

Index

A